# RIDERS OF A CERTAIN AGE

## Your Guide for Loving Horses Midlife and Beyond

# FRAN SEVERN

TRAFALGAR SQUARE
North Pomfret, Vermont

First published in 2022 by
Trafalgar Square Books
North Pomfret, Vermont 05053

**Disclaimer of Liability**
The author and publisher shall have neither liability nor responsibility to any person or entity with respect to any loss or damage caused or alleged to be caused directly or indirectly by the information contained in this book. While the book is as accurate as the author can make it, there may be errors, omissions, and inaccuracies.

Trafalgar Square Books encourages the use of approved safety helmets in all equestrian sports and activities.

**Library of Congress Cataloging-in-Publication Data**
Names: Severn, Fran, author.
Title: Riders of a certain age : your guide for loving horses midlife and beyond / Fran Severn.
Description: North Pomfret, Vermont : Trafalgar Square Books, 2022. |
    Includes bibliographical references and index. | Summary: "A delightfully honest look at the realities of starting out with horses...when you're getting older. Surveys show that riders over the age of 40 are the fastest-growing segment of the horse world, with those age 65 and above seeing the biggest jump. When we conjure up images of "horse girls" the picture is generally comprised of happily grubby youngsters or teenagers with roomsful of ribbons, but there is healthy segment of the equestrian population that first finds-or first finds time for-horses in mid-life or beyond. And this is the only handbook available for these riders, trainers, rescuers, and volunteers. With carefully curated guidance collected over years of horsing around, rider and writer Fran Severn wants readers to feel emboldened and empowered by the tips, lessons, and advice shared in these pages"-- Provided by publisher.
Identifiers: LCCN 2021049437 (print) | LCCN 2021049438 (ebook) | ISBN 9781646010493 (paperback) | ISBN 9781646010509 (epub)
Subjects: LCSH: Horsemanship for middle-aged persons. | Horsemanship for older people.
Classification: LCC SF309.26.M53 S48 2022  (print) | LCC SF309.26.M53 (ebook) | DDC 798.2084/6--dc23/eng/20211201
LC record available at https://lccn.loc.gov/2021049437
LC ebook record available at https://lccn.loc.gov/2021049438

Book design by Lauryl Eddlemon
Cover design by RM Didier
Index by Michelle Guiliano, DPM (linebylineindexing.com)
Typefaces:  Minion Pro; Acumin Pro

Printed in the United States of America
10 9 8 7 6 5 4 3 2 1

To Skip Webster, who taught me that
"rewrite" is not a dirty word, to always move the
story forward, and to drink Mai Tais when you win
an Emmy—a better friend and mentor
than he will ever know.

# CONTENTS

# The Making of a Rider of a Certain Age

**M**y mother's eldest sister, Aunt Alice (and that's the British "Ahhnt," not the American "Ant") was A Horsewoman, and don't you forget it! She had a farm in Maryland's hunt country north of Baltimore and lived the glamorous life of steeplechases and jumping, silver julep cups, and well-cut jodhpurs. There's a photo of me all of three years old in one of those fussy crinoline dresses that children wore on Sundays in the 1950s. I'm sitting on her black and white pony and waving uncertainly from the saddle. I know this was the first time I'd been on a horse. It was probably the first time I'd seen one.

A few years later, Aunt Alice sold the farm. Growing up in Baltimore City, the only horses I saw after that day were the ponies that hauled the fruit and vegetable wagons through the neighborhoods. But that brief encounter must have infected me because I fixated on horses. My nonexistent artistic skills drew barely recognizable pictures of horse heads. I covered my bedroom walls and bookshelves with posters and figurines of horses. I dreamed of moving to Montana and living on a ranch.

Instead, I went to college and earned a degree in Mass Communications. I movcd to Ohio where I worked at a TV station during the week. On weekends, I worked at the stables at Ogelbay Park in Wheeling, West Virginia, in exchange for accompanying the public trail rides. I turned down a career-enhancing job in Dayton, Ohio, for a stagnating position in Louisville, Kentucky, because, well— *Louisville*. I bought a half-blind rescued mare who took better care of me than I deserved as we trotted over jumps and rode through the woods. I got a new job at "the 50,000-Watt, clear channel voice of WHAS-Louisville" as a radio reporter and anchor. Best perk of that: covering the Kentucky Derby behind the scenes. My first Derby found me standing at the paddock gate and screaming as Affirmed and Alydar charged past us to the finish line. My last was watching Genuine Risk power past the stallions on her way to the blanket of roses.

My Air Force husband was transferred to New Mexico, and I hauled my aging gray mare from the lush Bluegrass to the arid High Plains. The look she gave me as she stepped off the trailer and saw nothing but scrub and tumbleweeds was one of disbelief and betrayal. But she served me well, carrying me safely through my pregnancy and becoming the favorite ride of the barn rats. When we transferred to England, she retired to her beloved Kentucky.

In England, I met Christine Dodwell, who introduced me to dressage. All her horses were trained to Prix St. George. None of them gave this uncoordinated, confused amateur any leeway. They always insisted that I perform every exercise properly and graced me with the gift of flowing movement and power when I asked correctly. When I wondered about Christine's willingness to put a thoroughly underprepared rider on such great horses, she said, "My dear, how will you know what you are trying to obtain if you do not experience it at the beginning?" She taught with kindness and understanding, always putting the horse and his needs before the rider's. That was perhaps her most valuable lesson. I took the British Horse Society's basic stable management class, marveling that I was paying some-one to teach me how to shovel…manure.

Then came the dark times of no horses. Returning to the States, I was back in Baltimore and swept up in family and career for 12 interminable years. When my husband got a job on Maryland's Eastern Shore, I did not think horses would be part of my new life there, either. The peninsula between the Chesapeake Bay and Atlantic Ocean is headquarters for much of the nation's commercial chicken farming industry. But to my shocked delight, I found horses there! Within a few weeks, I connected with an instructor and was back in the saddle, concentrating on dressage and natural horsemanship.

For the first time, I was able to spend all day around horses. Riding, training, helping with barn chores, attending clinics. Pure heaven! I even got a job at the local tack shop. We joked that our paychecks were simply an employee reinvestment program for the store. I bought a sweet chestnut Thoroughbred/Selle Français mare, a truck, and a trailer. We competed in local dressage shows, traveled to weekend camping trips, participated in clinics and workshops from Florida to New Hampshire. She gave me a lovely foal. The plan was that as my mare got older, I'd bring the colt along and let her relax into semi-retirement. Fate had other plans, and I lost the foal at 14 months to a freak medical condition.

Luckily, I'd bought a big Dutch Warmblood with the personality of a Labrador Retriever while my mare was in foal. I didn't have time for two horses, so the mare went to the teenager who had been leasing her. Love all around. A few years later, my big guy was retired and spent his last six years lounging with his friends and playing uncle to the young colts.

I found a new horse, this time a dignified Holsteiner who had somehow ended up in a rescue, then been adopted out to a hunter-jumper barn. The gelding's heart was in dressage, and his owner was happy to see him finally find the "right" home. More than teaching me riding skills and sharing trail rides through woods and snow and along beaches, he became a trusted companion. He got me through cancer and chemo and the loss of dearest friends before the curse of EPM claimed him.

Horses are anything but cheap, and my communications skills and media training helped me cover the inevitable bills. My fascination about everything in the horse world and my eagerness to share the knowledge soon had me writing for horse-oriented magazines, developing marketing materials and websites for riding schools and clubs, and organizing workshops and seminars about equine subjects. As I met more and more women my age who were also finally living their dream, I saw the need for filling their knowledge gap as I filled my own. We shared the same concerns about our bodies, minds, finances, and future. Magazine articles and social media posts just skimmed the surface. I started making notes, clicking on links, contacting experts, and scribbling rough drafts of book chapters. My answers were their answers. The result was this book.

Working on the book let me meet many inspiring women from all over the country and beyond. We've shared stories, advice, worries, heartbreak, jokes, and joys. The sisterhood of horsewomen is unlike any other sorority I know. We bond through love of our horses and know that anyone who loves her horse is someone worth having in our lives. I'm honored that you are letting me be part of your life and equine family.

# The Rider of a Certain Age

Does your head swivel when you drive past a field of grazing horses? Do you want Budweiser to bring back the ads with the Clydesdales? Does a dude ranch vacation sound more appealing than a Caribbean cruise?

Yep. You're a horse person. You are not alone. Horse ownership and horseback riding are increasingly popular pastimes. Every year, an estimated seven million people ride horses in the United States. Local riding clubs and casual groups of friends saddle up and hit the trail whenever they can. There's a horse show, gymkhana, hunt, or rodeo somewhere every weekend. The lure of buying a trailer with living quarters and traveling around the country to explore parks and trails appeals to many people.

And while online ads and catalogs feature trendy young models, we older gals with more classic styling are now recognized as a force in the equine world. Surveys show that riders over the age of 40 are the fastest-growing segment of the horse world, with those of us age 65 and above seeing the biggest jump. Since "60 is the new 40," finding women in their 70s sitting in the saddle is almost routine.

Some of us are lucky enough to have ridden since we wore diapers. For many more, though, horses were not part of our daily lives. Maybe you rode when you were a kid, but life, school, marriage, jobs, family, and finances forced you out of the saddle. Or your kids rode, so you became the stable mom who put their interests before your own, and now it's your turn. You might have been a city kid who never got closer to horses than the pony rides at the state fair. You read horse books and collected figurines, but, by and large, horses were a daydream, an ignored obsession that fell into that "someday" category. But horses were always there, nibbling at the edges of your wish list like a pony nibbling along the edges of the fence line.

Now, your life is changing. Your kids are grown, your career is winding down, your finances are stable (pun intended because that's where your money will be going), and your time is your own. You're ready to breathe in the sweet scent of fresh hay and horsehair and live your dream.

For many of us, there's a huge knowledge gap. We are smart women, not likely to start a new activity without learning how to do it well. Whether a newcomer to the horse world or a returning rider, you may have dozens of questions. Or, you might not even have enough experience to know what questions to ask, and you worry that you'll look foolish when you ask them. But while there are dozens of books, magazines, websites, and videos about horse training and riding techniques, none of them address things that specifically concern us, we "riders of a certain age."

We have issues that are alien to younger riders. For example, instructors are easy to find but do they understand the needs of older female riders? Most of them work with students who aren't dealing with menopause, unreliable urinary tracts, and stiff joints. Fear and insecurity are big worries for our age group. The ground seems much farther away and harder now than it did a decade or two ago. Our families are often unsupportive and suggest that we are being silly or selfish. We frequently struggle with trying to squeeze in time at the stable with home and work obligations. Our financial concerns are very different from those of younger women: pensions, Social Security, and retirement income often create limits for our dreams.

Social media explores a lot of what we need to know. Dozens of online groups are dedicated to the interests of older women who are discovering or rediscovering horses. The same questions, comments, and discussions appear regularly on all of them: how to find a trainer, how to get fit, how to deal with medical conditions, how to handle fear of riding, how to find a horse, how to choose the best protective gear, how to set up your own place, how to juggle job and family commitments with time at the barn, how to deal with an unsupportive spouse, how to travel and live on the road with your horse, and how to pay for it all.

*Riders of a Certain Age* fills in those gaps. You'll learn what you need to know before you climb into the saddle, like how to find the right instructor. Our high-mileage bodies require special attention to meet the demands of both aging and riding, so there are chapters about fitness, exercise, illness, and physical conditions. You'll find advice on dealing with the not-unreasonable fears that come with putting yourself on the back of a very large creature who thinks and communicates in his own language. There are strategies for winning over families who don't share your enthusiasm. Unless you retired with hefty stock options or won the Powerball, money is always an issue, so you'll acquire strategies for budgeting and paying the bills. These include deciding on buying a horse (or not) and what stuff you need to buy (and don't) to enjoy a happy riding lifestyle.

You'll find resources at the back of the book—leads to find groups, events, equipment, and horse-oriented activities, popular titles for books about building confidence and personal fitness, and where to download worksheets for budgeting (see p. 225). By and large, specific social media groups, products, or manufacturers are not mentioned. That's because things change rapidly in the horse world. Something listed today may be gone tomorrow while a great new resource has now appeared. You'll find the most current information and links on the book's companion website: www.ridersofacertainage.com. The Facebook page and group (RidersofaCertainAge) are also active for news and discussions.

So pull on your favorite breeches (ignoring the cellulite that manages to pucker through the Lycra), embrace your inner cowgirl, and proudly announce your status as one of the Riders of a Certain Age.

# PART ONE

## GETTING STARTED

# CHAPTER 1

# Women and Horses:
# Why and How We Love Them

**W**hat is it with women and horses? Why are so many women obsessed with horses, riding, and all things equine? With so many other activities available, what draws us to these great, sometimes mysterious beasts? Other people are dedicated to their hobbies, but not like us. Foursomes meet regularly to play a round of golf; Mahjong and bridge clubs toss tiles and bid fiercely every week. Some women attend their Zumba and aqua-aerobic classes with an almost religious fervor. But they rarely reach the level of total dedication that identifies horse lovers. And it seems to be an all-or-nothing fascination. You are either born with this disposition for loving horses, or you are, at best, disinterested. Those who don't share our passion don't understand it, or us. And we don't understand them.

There is little scientific research that explores why so many women love horses. Freud said it had to do with sexuality and how women really want to be men, but with Freud, everything had to do with sexuality and women wanting to be men.

To be fair, there are fundamental differences between the physiological and psychological makeup of men and women. Women have a deeper limbic system.

That's the part of our brains that controls behavior and emotions. Our limbic system predisposes us to be concerned with bonding, reproduction, feeding, sheltering, and protecting those under our care. Our female brains are wired to be more intuitive and emotional. We are generally more empathic than men, and we pick up non-verbal cues and body language much more easily than they do. The guys are hard-wired for domination and action. Empathy is generally viewed as a weakness, and intuition is often written off in favor of concrete, provable evidence. Where horses are concerned, by and large, women prefer trail riding, dressage, or working with rescues, while men gravitate toward high-energy competition like rodeo sports or three-day events. One comparison often heard is that women love horses, while men love riding.

Scientific research that explores equine attraction focuses on teenage girls and young adults, not mature women. Those studies found that while we may be moving toward a more gender-equal society, traditional stereotypes remain strong where horses are concerned. Horses are considered "girly," hence the popularity of My Little Pony and rainbow-bedecked unicorns. There's also the romantic notion of the White Knight galloping on his fiery steed to rescue the princess and living happily ever after.

Digging deeper for more substantive motivations, researchers find that horses provide a positive outlet for emotions that are often hard for girls to express. While boys have sports and assertive male role models, girls are pressured to be subservient and conform to other people's ideas of how they should live, think, and behave. For them, horses represent independence, strength, adventure, and accomplishment. Horses are non-judgmental and accepting as girls struggle to develop their own sense of self and deal with expectations and criticisms in school and at home. They provide both a deep emotional release and a sense of protection. Even girls who have no access to horses in their daily lives, like those growing up in cities, still dream of horses. They fill that "horse hole" with daydreams, Breyer models, movies, and pages of doodles of horses.

New research finds an intriguing physiological bond between horses and humans. Every living creature has an electromagnetic field. The field affects the brain waves of those near it. The horse's strongest electromagnetic field can be detected 20 feet away. The frequency is close to a human's "Alpha" frequency, which is the most relaxed and calmest mental state for humans. That may explain why just being around horses relaxes people. Our level of cortisol, the stress hormone, drops, and the level of endorphins, the "feel-good" hormones, rises. In one study of 18- to 30-year-olds, participants showed more patience, calmness, focus, self-esteem, and assertiveness after performing tasks as simple as bringing horses in from the field, grooming, and walking them around the paddock on a lead line.

This ability to project that calming natural strength is one reason why horses are so effective in treating people with post-traumatic stress disorder (PTSD) and other traumas. Trainers like Buck Brannaman, Chris Irwin, and Monty Roberts, who all had traumatic childhoods, acknowledge the healing effects of working with horses. Anecdotally, participants at clinics or training programs often share stories of trauma and abuse and how they were drawn to horses, even many years after the events.

In the horse world, "collection" refers to that moment when the horse and rider are one in terms of balance, flexibility, understanding, and sensitivity. Perhaps as adults, we find that horses represent the same powerful desires and sense of protection that attract young girls. A partnership with horses extends that "collection" into their riders' daily lives.

## LOVING HORSES ON THE GROUND

For most of us, getting involved with horses fulfills a lifelong dream of riding. We're eager to climb into the saddle and enjoy an adventure on the trail or dancing in a dressage arena. We want to try our hand at Western pleasure or bounce over a jump course.

Some of us, however, choose to enjoy horses with our feet planted firmly on the ground. Physical and emotional problems sometimes rule out safe or comfortable riding. Others find that the finances of lessons and equipment are prohibitive. Work and family obligations that leave no time for riding confront many women. Some question the ethics of putting horses under saddle, while others love horses but simply do not enjoy riding. Regardless of the reason, they share a common desire to enjoy a different and equally satisfying way of building a relationship with their horse.

The growing number of people who identify with those concepts inspired the "non-ridden equine" movement. The scattered practitioners began to find each other in 2017. That's when Victoria Yates started the Non-Ridden Equine Facebook page. When her horse, Kez, developed physical issues that ended his riding days, she decided to spend time with him out of the saddle rather than look for another riding partner. Word about the group spread, and there are now over 20,000 members.

Non-riders concentrate on spending time with their horse, mule, donkey, or Mini enjoying him as a companion animal, playing ground games, or participating in other activities. All horses, ridden or not, need to learn basic rules for being handled and groomed, brought in for feeding, vet checks, and dental and farrier work. Many non-riders and their horses go beyond this to enjoy perfecting more advanced skills. Horses learn in-hand jumping and dressage, coping with field and ground obstacles, and mastering tricks like bowing or standing on a circus pedestal. Dedicated teams perfect these skills at liberty. Horse Agility is a fairly new sport that is the equine version of the popular sport of dog agility. Human and horse teams navigate around, under, over, and through an obstacle course at liberty. It's ideal for riders who want to compete but not under saddle, and for horses that can't participate in ridden events for whatever reason. The International Horse Agility Club holds virtual competitions online.

Some women work at sanctuaries or rescues or turn their farms into retirement homes or shelters. They rehabilitate horses rescued from situations of neglect or abuse, devoting their time and effort to rebuilding the health and trust of the horses in their care. Depending on the facility, they might be involved in training a horse for adoption or learning to care for a special needs horse who will remain there for life. Others turn their farm into a business opportunity by hosting special programs like writer retreats, seminars on equine photography, or yoga, reiki, and meditation weekends. Some B & Bs include interactive horse experiences as part of their package. Other stables welcome school groups to learn about horses and farm life. Well-trained and reliable horses occasionally visit patients in nursing homes and hospitals. Driving horses in carts and traps is enjoying a revival of interest for pleasure, competition, and business.

Therapy is a strong theme in the non-ridden equine world. Equine-assisted therapy taps into horses' unique behavior and understanding to help people dealing with PTSD and emotional and mental trauma. EAGALA (Equine Assisted Growth and Learning Association) and the Equine Experiential Education Association certify individuals to work with licensed professionals in a wide-ranging scope of therapies.

Programs for at-risk kids use horses to instill confidence and a sense of acceptance in a positive, supportive setting. Personal development, corporate training, and team-building programs frequently use horses to facilitate their activities.

If they have the acreage, some of those deeply interested in the natural horse world create environments that encourage horses to roam and graze on the move as they would in the wild by strategically placing watering areas throughout the property and planting native flora instead of lush pastures. This "Paddock Paradise" concept is a small, but growing, phenomenon. There is at least one university that is incorporating it into its Equine Behavior and Herd Management program (see more about this in the reference section—p. 225).

While the established horse world might still think that riding is the primary reason for owning a horse, the non-ridden opportunities prove that there is a lot of enjoyment and satisfaction far beyond the saddle.

## CRUISES, VACATIONS, AND OTHER ADVENTURES

When horses become the center of your life, you want to work them into all your plans. Your daily schedule adjusts to accommodate riding, chores, and visits to the feed store. You collect saddle pads the way you once shopped for shoes and makeup. Forget chick flicks and romance novels. Unless horses are featured, or the story is set on a ranch, you aren't interested.

You subscribe to equine magazines, join horse-oriented social media groups, and an evening of online shopping leaves you with a melted credit card and a 16-hand-high stack of UPS boxes on your porch.

Our passion quite naturally extends into our leisure time. Who wants an ocean cruise when the only equines present are seahorses? No problem! Cruise lines know that people who are passionate about their interests love to combine cruising amenities while meeting others who share their interests. Ocean cruises market trips for knitters and cat lovers, and on nostalgia cruises, passengers move to the beat with nightly performances by rock stars from the seventies. Horse lovers are another welcome special-interest group. Equine enthusiasts take a break from winter chores on week-long cruises in the Caribbean, stopping at ports in Mexico and the islands. Some of the cruises are structured affairs and include seminars, films, and educational programs. Others are more of a week-long floating party for horse lovers. They enjoy the pools, buffets, spas, entertainment, and casinos available to all passengers, but with special activities like group dinners and happy hours. On both themed and non-themed cruises, most offer horseback riding excursions with rides along the beach and in the sea.

You can immerse yourself in the life of the Old West. Join wranglers on a working cattle ranch and help round up a herd in the high mesas of New Mexico and drive them to winter pastures at dude and guest ranches. Learn roping and reining; ride a Mustang through the quaking Aspens in Colorado. Or pamper yourself at a luxury guest ranch. Intersperse rides with spa treatments, exquisite dining, and elegant accommodations. Many ranches schedule "girlfriend getaway" and adult-only weeks. Those can be as laid-back as trail rides with wine coolers around the pool in the afternoon or a strenuous, all-women cattle drive. While most ranches are in the western United States and Canada, you'll find some in Florida, Virginia, New York, Georgia, and Ohio. The Dude Ranchers Association website filters for location, riding options, lodging, food, and activities other than riding.

If you went to a summer camp that offered horseback riding or were one of the lucky girls who went to a camp that was all about riding, you can return to those days or discover them for the first time. Some stables offer week-long riding camps for grownups. Along with games, lessons, and trail rides, riders enjoy cookouts and socializing in the evening after finishing chores. Accommodations are on-site in a bunkhouse, RVs, or at local hotels or B&Bs.

History lovers merge their love for all things old with their love of horses by joining reenactor groups. Mounted units portray the lives of cavalry units from the Revolutionary and Civil Wars. Many of them include women in their ranks as both riders and trainers. For the more fanciful riders, the Society for Creative Anachronism, a group dedicated to medieval pursuits, celebrates the age with jousting and archery on horseback and grand parades with ladies in Maid Marian finery. Riding troupes celebrating Mexican, Tejano, and Native American heritage welcome riders who share those roots.

When traveling, destinations often have trail rides, stable tours, or local horse-oriented entertainment. Tour companies specializing in equine package tours combine riding with sightseeing. Depending on your interest, you can join a safari in Africa, ride the Outback in Australia, study dressage in Germany or Spain, go fox hunting in the Irish countryside, or join a week-long trek across Scotland from the North Sea to the Irish Sea. Some riding schools in Europe accept students for lessons lasting from a few days to several months. Several tour companies offer "women only" trips. You'll meet riding buddies scattered across the country and the world who share your love of horses and adventure.

Weekend retreats with horses as a backdrop or integral to the itinerary are another way to expand your group of friends while developing new skills or enjoying other hobbies. Popular programs focus on yoga or mindful horsemanship. Other weekend clinics address fear of riding with participants supporting and encouraging each other in ways they often do not find in their daily lives. Some combine riding with Bible study and spiritual reflection. Photography seminars are hugely popular; who doesn't want to learn how to take fabulous photos of their horses and nature? Poetry and journaling workshops encourage you to take pen to paper to find your creative muse. The possibilities for equine entertainment and adventure away from the stable are endless.

# CHAPTER 2

# Finding an Instructor: It's Like Looking for the Perfect Partner

You've embraced your inner Dale Evans. You are ready to learn how to saddle up, post, lope, use a curry comb, and clean out stalls. You're as giddy as a kid on Christmas morning. You are going to be a rider, a horsewoman!

Setting goals for this adventure is important. Spend some time thinking about why you want to ride. Obviously, the first goal is to have fun and do something enjoyable and exciting. But what is it about becoming a rider that attracts you more than other hobbies? Informal discussions on forums and chat rooms produce many reasons. You enjoy learning something new and take pride in your accomplishments. Riding is a fun form of fitness, far more exciting and relaxing than using a treadmill or joining a "senior aerobics" class at the gym. It's a new lifestyle with new people to add as friends. There's an almost spiritual attraction to the power, wonder, and aura of horses.

Those are all general reasons. What you specifically want to do in the saddle might be harder to define. Right now, that might not be more than "riding." You may be at the "Dick and Jane" stage of your equestrian knowledge. You know that

English and Western riding have different saddles and that English riders wear breeches and safety helmets while Western riders sport jeans and Stetsons. Beyond that, it's an alien world.

On the other hand, maybe you've always harbored a secret desire to pop over obstacles in a hunter-jumper course or try to break 18 seconds in a barrel race. You daydream about moseying along a tree-lined path through a forest or galloping through the surf on a beach. Perhaps you want to compete and hang a few ribbons on the wall or go camping with your horse. As you look toward retirement, you might consider buying some land and keeping a few horses. Or, maybe you'll travel around the country with your horse, staying at parks and campgrounds near riding trails.

Those goals will probably change, particularly if you are new to riding, but having some idea of where you might want to end up helps you know where to start. A riding instructor plays a significant role in that journey.

An instructor is the person who will give you the knowledge to build the foundation for a long, happy, safe, and successful adventure with horses. She helps you discover your abilities, gives you confidence, encourages your learning, and motivates both you and the horse in your life (which could be a lesson horse, a leased horse, or your own horse—I'll talk about all of these in the pages ahead). She teaches you the basics of horse care and safe horse handling. If owning a horse is on your agenda, she can lead the search for your best partner.

Tracking down such a wizard takes time and effort. Lucky individuals find a great riding stable and instructor right away. Others ride with several people before they find someone who "clicks." A teaching approach that's brilliant for one rider may totally fail with another. You'll find that the "best" instructor is different for each person. And, as you develop your skills and change your interests, you will probably work with several instructors.

Your community may be blessed with lots of stables and a number of instructors. On the other hand, you may not have many choices. It is frustrating when you want to learn how to rein but live in hunter-jumper country. However, it is more important to find someone who is competent overall than one who focuses primarily on the details of a particular discipline. As a beginner or returning rider, you need to learn or refresh the *basics* of riding, and those are the same no matter what kind of saddle you use. Balance, aids, "feel," understanding horse behavior, and safe handling of horses are universal.

When looking for an instructor, word of mouth is a good start. If you already have contacts in the local riding community, ask for recommendations. Visit local feed stores and tack shops and ask about stables and instructors. Someone at the store probably takes lessons herself or knows the local instructors. Look for the free local magazines distributed at feed stores and tack shops. They contain ads for stables, instructors, clinics, shows, and classifieds selling tack, trailers, and horses. Stables and riding clubs often post flyers on store bulletin boards. Attend horse shows. Wander around the trailers and hang out at the warm-up rings. Listen to the instructors as they coach their students, and watch the students as they ride.

Most states have a Horse Council or similar industry association or an equine office within the state's Agriculture Department. They frequently maintain lists of riding clubs. Another option is to search the websites of breed and special interest groups like the Arabian Horse Association, American Quarter Horse Association, or the US Dressage Federation, as examples. National groups have regional chapters and can give you leads on instructors in your geographical location and area of interest.

And, as mentioned already, there are many groups on social media platforms specifically for older women riders. They often have geographic directories, so you can connect with local riders and ask for recommendations (see p. 225).

## THE QUALITIES OF A GOOD INSTRUCTOR

People teach for many reasons. For some, it is the foundation of their business. For others, it's a sideline to support their own training and competition. Others are part-time instructors with "normal" jobs who teach to pick up some extra cash. Any one of them can be excellent or awful. Not all riders, even those with a wall covered with blue ribbons, are talented teachers.

All instructors, even the poor ones, can teach the basics. After all, it's not hard to explain neck reining or posting diagonals. But a good instructor possesses other qualities. She should start at your level of ability and confidence, be even-natured, quiet but enthusiastic. She should be confident but not arrogant. And perhaps the most important quality of all, she should never stop trying to make riding and learning fun!

These traits are important no matter who she is teaching, but there are other concerns instructors must address when working with an older rider. One of the most important is understanding our physical limitations, mental functions, and emotional uncertainty. At most stables, the age group of the riders is skewed toward teenagers and a smattering of 20- to 30-somethings. They know the jargon of the horse world and are comfortable with the routines of a stable. You, meanwhile, may not know the difference between the pastern and the poll or what "holding the horse for the farrier" means. They jump into the saddle with ease while you awkwardly hoist yourself with a death grip on the pommel. They move with coordination and flexibility while you gimp to your car after your lesson and look for the ibuprofen in your glove compartment.

Instructors always seek new clients, and older riders are a potential source of new business. Some stables are devoted "lesson barns" with "schoolmaster" horses to learn general riding skills on. Others may focus on serious competition, may be firmly locked into one discipline, or may require you have your own horse. Those stables that offer a wide range of classes and activities are generally welcoming. Some go so far as to have adult-only group lessons and activities, including after-lesson Happy Hours, trail rides, "Girls Only" weekends, and non-riding social outings. They recognize that friends and companionship are two of the main reasons why women, particularly older women, ride.

These instructors also appreciate our attitudes. Many of them say that older riders are their easiest and most enjoyable students. We often treat our instructors more respectfully and professionally than other students. We focus on making ourselves better riders. Almost universally, we are hard workers who want a good grounding in the basics of riding and horse care. We want to be safe and have fun. We expect to get our money's worth and are willing to put in the effort that requires. Most of us are not in a hurry to meet some goal, which makes for a more relaxed learning environment for both our instructor and us. More so than younger riders, we enjoy the nuances of understanding how to communicate with our horses and the theory behind the cues and the exercises. The instructors recognize that many of us lack confidence and are often even frightened of riding, but that we are determined to work through that. They work with us to overcome the fear and find the joy. In addition to classes, we boost our equine knowledge by reading, watching educational videos, and attending clinics.

In general, instructors find that competition is not high on our bucket list, although participating in low-level local shows is an exciting accomplishment. More commonly, we want to saddle up for a trail ride or work on developing better riding skills for the sheer enjoyment and sense of accomplishment in doing so. Fitness is a concern, particularly for those of us who've not been diligent in that area. A few instructors require students to follow a fitness plan as part of their riding program. Most, however, encourage riders to work on physical conditioning and weight control independently.

Communication skills are just as necessary as technical knowledge. While your instructor can be as patient as a Buddhist monk, if you don't understand what she is trying to explain, you're wasting both your time and your money. Asking questions and giving feedback result in a better lesson for all three of you, rider, instructor, and horse. Your instructor needs to know that you understand the exercise, terms, and reason you are doing something. Don't be polite and say "yes" if you genuinely don't. Speak up if you are confused. If you don't say anything, your instructor will think you are doing well when you might be lost.

The keys to good communication include your instructor being clear and flexible with her explanations. When verbal directions fail, she adds visual and sensory examples. She might suggest, "You should feel like you're holding no more than a stick of butter" to explain hands that are soft on the reins and gentle on the horse's mouth. Or both of you might hold reins while she demonstrates what the horse is feeling from the bit. Or she may create visual prompts like telling you to mentally align a zipper up the front of your jacket to prevent you from leaning to either side. Simply repeating the same directions, either quietly and calmly or with increasing exasperation, is not good communication.

A flexible mindset is another vital talent for instructors. For example, the lesson plan for the day is clear, and you and your instructor know the day's goal. The arena is ready with all equipment in place. But once the lesson starts, something is off. You can't find your balance, or your horse keeps shying at a barrel in the corner of the ring. A good instructor is flexible enough to switch gears and make dealing with those issues the focus of the lesson. She should also be sharp enough to determine if the day's problems are just a glitch or if they are a signal that there are holes in the training (either yours or the horse's or both) and that future lessons might need to shift their focus to address them.

Sometimes, she'll push you to move along faster than you want, which often comes from your desire to do everything perfectly. That's a common trait after years of successfully managing everything from a household to a business. We've forgotten that making mistakes is part of the learning process. If you don't move outside of your comfort zone, both you and the horse you ride will soon be frustrated and bored. On the other hand, you don't want shortcuts, especially with the basics. If you truly feel uncomfortable with the pace of learning, either too fast or too slow, talk it over with your instructor. You both need to be comfortable with the lesson plans.

## CREDENTIALS

In the United States, there is no defined professional or educational path for someone who wants to instruct students or train horses. (This is different in other countries, such as Germany and England.) Unlike other professions, riding instruction and horse training have no required or recognized certification or licensing procedures. Only Massachusetts requires licensing for horseback riding instructors.

However, there are several voluntary professional certification programs. If your instructor is certified by The Certified Horsemanship Association, American Riding Instructors Association, US Hunter-Jumper Association, Centered Riding, US Dressage Federation, or the British Horse Society, it shows competency, dedication, and professional intent. (The websites for each of these groups have geographic directories of instructors.)

There are also certification programs from well-known clinicians and instructors. Again, websites for these programs often have geographical listings of instructors.

Dozens of colleges offer two- to four-year certification and degree programs in equine studies. However, few offer any courses in how to teach riding. They focus on horse training, horse care, and the business side of the equine industry. An instructor with such a degree is clearly dedicated to a professional career in the field, although teaching is probably not her primary focus.

Many professional trainers, competitors, and instructors offer working student positions. The students often tend to the horses and perform barn chores in exchange for a smidgen of pay, living accommodations, and a few lessons a week. The hours are usually long and the physical demands heavy, but—depending on the stable—the learning and professional opportunities are excellent. At some stables, working students offer lessons under the supervision of the more experienced instructors.

Whether or not she has certification of some kind, a good instructor continues her education and refines her skills by attending clinics and riding with more experienced professionals.

Every instructor has her own approach to teaching and different goals for herself and her students. Some instructors are very traditional in their approach. They apply teachings from famous trainers and competitors and rely on long-established methods for both rider and horse. Others lean toward "natural" systems, which emphasize equine psychology. Some instructors have a tack room full of equipment and artificial aids; others prefer less mechanical methods. Some instructors want to see quick results; others are not concerned about timetables.

Keep in mind that the background does not reflect the quality of the instructor. Just because someone competes successfully and trains her own horses doesn't mean she's a good teacher. Not everyone has the skills or ability to effectively communicate their equine knowledge and experience to students.

The cost of lessons is not a good indication of quality, either. The fee reflects the instructor's reputation and experience, your geographic location, the stable's facilities, and the focus of the riding program (showing, beginners, kids, casual riders, intense training, serious amateurs). In the English riding world, the joke is that you should expect to pay an extra $10 an hour if the instructor wears high-end name-brand equestrian clothing, another $10 if the instructor has a European accent, and yet another $20 if that instructor is also male. In the Western world, the price rises according to the size of the instructor's hat and belt buckle, and the brand of her boots. In reality, the only thing that matters is that you find the best instructor you can afford.

## EVALUATING A POTENTIAL INSTRUCTOR

Once you have the names of a few possible instructors, give them a call. Tell them where you are in your riding journey and what you are looking for. It's fine if those goals are not much beyond just wanting to ride, have fun, and learn about horses. Be realistic about your abilities, what you know, and what you can (and can't) do. What you did when you were a child probably no longer applies. Let her know your concerns about starting or returning to riding as an adult. Most instructors are supportive and try to be accommodating. They want you to enjoy yourself and become a regular client (and a reliable revenue source).

Ask if she is comfortable with new or low-level riders and, if necessary, has lesson horses for you to ride. Ask if she has other older students.

If you have physical limitations, ask if she can work around them. As already mentioned, she needs to understand the biomechanics and physical limitations of older riders, and she may need to expand her knowledge base to serve your needs. It's a good sign if she knows about Pilates, chiropractic treatments, yoga, and other exercise therapies that help your riding. Ultimately, though, it is up to you to monitor and determine your abilities and limitations.

Does her program have a particular emphasis? If you are new to riding, you probably want to find a place that focuses more on having fun while learning than perfecting professional-level skills. On the other hand, if your dream is to ride Prix St. George at Dressage at Devon or compete in reining at the AQHA Regional Championships, a stable that's big on pony camps and weekend pleasure rides is probably not a good fit, either.

If the conversation goes well, schedule a visit to the stable to see if the people and the place are right for you. Evaluate a lesson. You may not know precisely what is happening, but you can get a good sense of the atmosphere.

You may decide that the first stable you try is a great fit. However, if you feel

# *Lesson Barn Evaluation*

➤ Is the riding area prepared for the lesson? Is all the equipment needed on hand and in place?

➤ Is the instructor focusing entirely on the lesson, or does she stop to deal with other barn issues, phone calls, and interruptions?

➤ Does she seem to enjoy teaching?

➤ Are the instructor and student comfortable with each other?

➤ Is the instructor patient?

➤ Is she asking for feedback, encouraging questions, and striving to clarify things when the student is confused?

➤ Is she flexible in explaining concepts and how to do things?

➤ Short-tempered, sarcastic, or belittling comments about the rider are a warning sign. Ditto if she makes snide remarks about other riders, trainers, or instructors.

➤ How many days a week does she teach, and when?

➤ Do you have a choice of group lessons, which are often less expensive, or private lessons? Many instructors want you to begin with private lessons so they can concentrate on teaching you the most important basics without distraction. Don't be put off by the prospect of riding with kids if that's an option. Their enthusiasm and joy are contagious.

➤ If riding a lesson horse, will you ride the same horse for each lesson, or will you ride different ones?

➤ If you already have a horse, will she ride and evaluate him? (She should *want* to do this so that she can learn his movements, quirks, and abilities.)

➤ Is she willing to ride your horse at other times (for an additional fee, of course) to work on training elements that are beyond your abilities or time?

*(continued)*

➤ Are you allowed to video lessons so you can review them on your own? Seeing what you are doing makes it easier to transfer those concepts into the saddle. Not all stables have that ability, but it's becoming a common option with the popularity of sports camera devices and video apps.

➤ When is payment due? Are there pre-pay packages of four or five lessons, perhaps for a discount? This is a good option. You'll rarely be able to decide if an instructor is right for you with just one lesson. Ride several times at one place before trying another. It takes a few lessons to get comfortable with the instructor and the rhythm of the program.

➤ What are the cancellation policies? These often seem harsh. However, clients are notorious for canceling at the last moment or just not showing up at all, which is, at best, rude. No-shows mean no income. No instructor will retire to Barbados on her income from teaching or running a boarding stable, so no-shows seriously damage her bottom line. As a result, they are strict about their payment plans.

okay but are not blown away, there's no reason not to try another instructor. Never worry about hurting the instructor's feelings if you don't sign on as a regular client. You are a customer. Consider it "test driving" many models of cars. You keep trying them until you find the right fit.

## BEING A GOOD STUDENT: MAKE YOUR INSTRUCTOR SMILE

You know what to expect from your instructor, but what can your instructor expect from you? You have responsibilities to her, the horse, and the other people at the stable if you want to be successful and safe, enjoy the experience, become a better rider, and fit in well with your new horsey family.

The first is to commit to time in the saddle. Even if your schedule and finances allow for only one lesson a week, make that lesson a rock-solid commitment.

Show up on time.

Be ready to start when the class begins. That does not mean pulling up to the barn a few minutes before the lesson time and breathlessly dashing into the riding ring, particularly if you are responsible for catching, grooming, and saddling your horse. Be prepared with whatever equipment you need. If the warm-up is not part of the lesson, you should have completed that by lesson time.

If you ride between lessons, do whatever homework your instructor assigned. If she did not give you specific suggestions, practice what you covered during your last ride. You might be confused by the new terms you hear for parts of the horse, saddle, and other equipment. Don't be embarrassed to ask for definitions. (And there's no shame in putting up a poster of the parts of the horse, saddles, and tack in your house. Buy a copy of the *Pony Club Manual of Horsemanship: Basics for Beginners/D Level.* You're playing "catch up" and are trying to learn what the "barn rat" kids have absorbed over years.)

If you are running late, have the courtesy to call ahead and give the instructor a heads-up. She may reschedule the lesson for later that day or suggest rescheduling it for another date. If not, don't expect her to extend your class time. You may have paid for an hour, but so has the next rider. Your instructor may have other plans for the remainder of the day, and your tardiness messes up her schedule. You may have to accept the loss of lesson time without a refund.

Make sure your instructor knows your limitations. If your physical conditions interfere with your lesson, tell her immediately. As older riders, our issues are not always obvious. It's hard to sit in the proper position or move with your horse when you have a stiff back or bad knees. Medications can affect your ability to concentrate, your coordination, and your balance. Hearing loss can cause problems in large spaces, particularly outside on a windy day. Your instructor needs to know what you can and can't do so that she can adjust the lesson to accommodate you.

One of your limitations may well be fear. One of our age group's biggest concerns is the incongruous situation of being very frightened of riding but absolutely refusing to stay away from horses. Many riders are embarrassed until they discover how many "mature" riders share these emotions. Most instructors are impressed at your determination and work hard to support you and give you confidence.

Leave your kids and pets at home. No, your dog will not get along with the other animals. Yes, he will chase the barn cat, quite possibly through the arena in the middle of a lesson. No, not all horses or people are comfortable around dogs. No, your kids or grandkids will not sit quietly doing their homework or harmlessly explore the barn during your lesson. Horses and farriers do not like small children running up behind them. Yes, other people at the stable do mind when you ask them to watch your kids or dog while you ride. They may be too polite to say so, but you can bet the instructor or barn manager will get an earful.

Pay attention. That means limiting distractions, which is another reason for leaving the kids and dogs at home. Nothing distracts from a lesson more than hearing a child scream followed by an ominous thud or a snarling dogfight in the parking area.

Turn off your phone. You are paying for information and techniques to make you a better rider. It is insulting to your instructor and her experience to check messages or your newsfeed or take selfies during the lesson.

If you have a group lesson, don't gab with the other riders while your instructor is working with someone else. Neither the other riders nor the instructor appreciates it. Since most group lessons involve people at roughly the same level of expertise, you can learn a lot by watching and listening.

Don't compare your instructor with other horse trainers or former riding instructors. Negative comments about them are impolite and unprofessional. Demanding to know why she doesn't use techniques that other instructors follow is equally out of line. If your instructor's approach is so very different from what you want to hear, you should probably find another instructor.

Don't blame the horse. If you are riding a lesson horse, he quite likely has been around since gasoline was $1.50 a gallon. There isn't a rider's mistake he hasn't seen, and there isn't a rider who hasn't learned from him. Just ask him politely, and he'll try for you.

You need to try for him, too. Your instructor will ask you to do things that are outside your comfort zone. That's her job, and that's the only way you learn. Your job is to give it your best effort.

Pay on time! Your payment is your instructor's paycheck. You expect to see your money on payday. So does she.

And most importantly, have fun!

## HOW WE LEARN: THINKING AND PHYSICAL SKILLS

You pull into the parking area by the barn, ready for your first lesson. You're giddy at the thought of grooming your lesson horse and sitting in the saddle. But inside, you are cringing. *Can I really do this? Can I learn something so radically "new" at my age? Am I smart enough and sharp enough both mentally and physically?*

Most of us haven't studied in a formal setting since we left school. Older adults returning to college as students or auditors are often overwhelmed as we relearn study habits. We are blindsided by the speed and intensity of classwork and the new technology of educational computing. Add in apps like Facebook, Pinterest, Twitter, and TikTok, not to mention "alphabet" shorthand, trending hashtags, and creative spellings that would have given our high school English teachers a stroke, and we long for the days when cassettes, VHS tapes, and floppy discs were hi-tech. If you feel like a fossil, you are not alone. According to Pew Research, 77 percent of seniors need help with technology.

Learning situations are easier to handle for those working in fields that require constant training and continuing education. New technology is introduced gradually, and you have time to adjust and learn how to use it. But when the classroom is a sand arena, and the tools and terms are unfamiliar, your comfort level sinks, no matter your background.

Even if you are comfortable with the idea of getting back into "learning mode," you might worry about your mental abilities overall. The specter of "senior moments" hovers at the back of your mind. Is forgetting to turn off the water hose at the barn a momentary blip or the first symptom of dementia?

While researchers spent years studying how children and young adults learn, our age group was ignored. Now that we are a sizeable share of the population (and maybe because many of these researchers are getting closer to Social Security age themselves), the cognitive abilities of people over 50 are analyzed in as much detail as the nutritional plan for a horse that's a "hard keeper." Dozens of studies in the last decade examine how we think, how we learn, and how our brains work in conjunction with our bodies.

The results are encouraging. Barring injury or illness, most of our cognitive abilities stay strong throughout our lives. Neuroscientists say that mentally active people keep their thinking skills better than those who are mentally sedentary. A trial group of adults age 65 and over participated in training sessions to improve memory, reasoning, and cognitive processing. After 10 sessions, mental skills improved and lasted for 10 years. Games—be they crossword puzzles, card games, or board games—are mental workouts, as are reading and participating in activities that require planning, like deciding what you will do in a riding session, planting a garden, or organizing a vacation trip. Even cleaning tack can be stimulating, particularly if you disassemble a complicated bridle and need to remember how to put it back together!

Mental activity creates a "cognitive reserve." This means you have the skills and experience to adapt and learn. Taking on challenging activities strengthens numerous networks within the brain. That stimulation may help prevent dementia and

Alzheimer's. Mentally active people can also cope better with the loneliness, stress, and depression that come after the loss of a spouse, close friend, or pet. Active people feel more positive about their abilities and the future. On the physical side, lifelong learning lowers stress levels, slows the heart rate, and encourages relaxation.

Several mental areas deteriorate somewhat as we age. These are primarily our ability to process information, our attention span, our reasoning ability, and our memory. Those areas operate in conjunction with each other. We may compensate for weakness in one area by drawing more on one of the stronger areas.

One of the most significant negative changes is the speed at which we process information. It slows measurably. We no longer instantly understand something. We might need to hear, read, or apply information several times. Once we do, however, the information is locked in. We also find it harder to focus and ignore distractions. We have shorter attention spans and struggle to multitask. Dovetailing with these, our physical reaction time also slows. We don't analyze and react to situations as quickly as we once did. This may be one reason why older people have more falls, and older drivers have more car accidents.

"Cognitive flexibility" is another feature that, like our joints, often becomes stiffer with age. This is summed up by the attitude of "My mind is made up; don't bother me with facts." We often resist new ideas, choosing instead to rely on past experiences or follow longstanding habits, rules, or beliefs that we find comfortable. To some extent, that's good because we have years of experience to draw upon. On the other hand, we might ignore new information or its source because it doesn't fit our mindset. We also lose some of our ability to draw inferences, like reading between the lines in a situation and making conclusions by reasoning. It's harder for us to juggle ideas when trying to solve a problem.

Researchers break memory down into many categories. A few of them decline with age. Those include remembering something without a hint. Abilities that stay strong are how to do things like ride a bicycle and the sequence in which to perform a task like hitching up a trailer. Language skills also stay strong, although we have more "tip of the tongue" experiences, which is a result of the need for more reminder cues and slower mental processing speed.

Just as they explore the working of our brains as we age, researchers also examine how our aging bodies perform physical tasks. We lose one-quarter of our muscle mass by age 60, one-half by age 80. That loss is associated with increased fragility, poor balance, and falls. Our general physical condition affects our motor skills, so using our bodies is key to maintaining strength, flexibility, and coordination.

Two areas of physical development that interest researchers are "movement learning" and "movement skill." Both of them affect our muscle movement, aka "motor skills."

There are two areas of muscle movement: gross motor skills and fine motor skills. Gross motor skills incorporate a great deal of muscular activity that involves the total body, like riding. Fine motor skills require minimal body movement but need good hand-to-eye coordination, like lacing our boots or refilling a spray bottle without using a funnel.

"Movement learning" means acquiring new skills and improving existing ones. Although our physical strength and performance decline as we age, our ability to create new or revive forgotten muscle memory remains strong. The rate of that learning slows significantly for adults over age 60 due to the general slowing of our mental processing. We need more time to perform a task because we do not organize our movements as efficiently as younger adults. In a new situation, we rely more on visual cues because we are not as finely aware of our bodies.

"Movement skill" is coordination. As we learn a new skill or refresh an old one, we initially move more slowly and less accurately as we think through each element. We need more time to practice, and we may never refine the skill as well as a younger person. But with repetition, it can become a smooth, natural activity. For example, consider the first time you stood on a mounting block. *Where do I stand?*

*How do I swing my leg over? How does my foot go into the stirrup? If I don't grab the horn, will I fall over the other side?* Mounting gets easier as you practice and gain confidence until you do it without thinking. But if you try to get on from the *other* side of the horse, you'll need to concentrate on each movement again because you have no muscle memory for that action.

Age-related effects on muscles are reversible to a point. Physical activity and strength training restores muscles, slows further decline, and helps strengthen bones. Adults between the ages of 60 and 80 with an exercise program can increase their aerobic fitness by as much as 30 percent, which is helpful when your horse decides to play tag when you try to catch him in the field.

## REMOTE LEARNING: WHAT TO DO WHEN THERE IS NO LOCAL INSTRUCTOR

What happens if you live in the back of beyond where there are no instructors, and you must learn on your own? Fortunately, through the wonders of technology, remote learning isn't all that remote anymore. Many options allow you to develop a thorough, effective training program. It usually will, however, require you have access to a horse—your own or perhaps a friend's.

Most people need a combination of visual, written, and oral information to learn. How much you need of each element varies depending on your personal formula for mental comprehension. Some of us need a carefully planned, step-by-step program with lots of explanations presented in multiple ways. Others have a talent for pulling information from several sources to develop their own coherent program. Still others are confident in their riding skills and need help only to address a particular training or riding issue. For some of us, reading a book and studying photographs provides all the direction we need. Whatever your learning style, a few hours online supplies you with an overwhelming number of suggestions and information.

### Home Study Courses

In the late 1990s, a then-unknown trainer named Pat Parelli and his then-wife Linda pioneered a new idea in horse training. They developed a complete study course for learning at home without an instructor. Before this, students learned by taking lessons, attending clinics, or on their own by trial-and-error.

Their concept used horse psychology as the fundamental of training, a system they called "Natural Horsemanship." None of the ideas were new; they just figured out how to condense the lessons from masters like Ray Hunt and Tom Dorrance into one program. The original course included a video, textbooks that explained their theories and principles, and pocket guides to illustrate the exercises. Within a few years, they introduced a more sophisticated and structured program. Residential courses opened at two locations. An online club allowed students to connect virtually. Parelli also began certifying trainers throughout the country to teach their program, which was another innovation in horse and rider training.

Although commonplace now, at the time, it was a game-changer. Other trainers, who either taught solely at their ranches or traveled around the country holding clinics, recognized the potential of reaching a larger audience and earning a better living, and copied the original idea. They began producing their own study programs, clinics, and certification programs. Home study programs now cover every level of ability and discipline of riding. Programs are available online and streaming on computers and mobile devices. Several clinicians have cable TV programs, dedicated YouTube channels, and membership programs that include podcasts and online group meetings.

Some courses teach riding beginning at a novice level and progress to expert. Others focus exclusively on one discipline, like reining or dressage. Some are designed for the absolute beginner who needs to be shown how to hold a lead rope. Others assume a certain level of experience. Many of them have online communities and often feature live chats with the instructor. Others offer video coaching or assessments. Most charge either a flat fee for the program or a monthly subscription.

Major horse expos, like Equitana, Equine Affaire, Western States Horse Expo, and Horse World Expo attract prominent clinicians. If you cannot attend the expos in person, view the event's schedule to see which riders and trainers sound interesting, and you can then visit their websites for more information.

### Virtual\Video Coaching

This is one of the fastest-growing areas of riding instruction. It combines a home study course with a remotely located instructor. You video your ride and send it to an instructor who reviews it and sends feedback. Although not as personal and immediate as working in person with an instructor, there are several advantages. You are not limited to local instructors. You can train with someone on the other side of the country or the other side of the world. You also avoid the inconvenience and expense of trailering to a stable or paying mileage on top of lesson fees to have an instructor come to you.

There are many variations on the concept. Some instructors offer a structured course with specific lesson plans. Other lessons are open-ended. The instructor evaluates your video, you review it together, and she provides suggestions. Depending on the technology, the instructor can even "draw" on the screen to highlight something, much like the way football commentators draw squiggles on the screen to illustrate a game. The newest innovation is live lessons. Using real-time technology like that used for remote meetings, the instructor can watch and teach as you ride.

There are two challenges to accomplishing successful virtual lessons. The first is finding an instructor. Spend a few evenings browsing through websites for those who offer virtual sessions. Make a chart that compares what sort of instruction is offered, the background of the instructor, how the videos are sent, how the feedback is delivered, whether the lessons are a structured course, if there is a minimum requirement for how many lessons you must take, the availability of the instructor and how frequently you can take a lesson, cancellation policies, and payment plans. Contact the instructors who interest you. Just as with a face-to-face meeting with a prospective instructor, let her know your experience, your goals, your age, and any physical limitations. Find out if she has experience working with older riders. Keep in mind that it is more challenging for a virtual instructor to adapt to your physical needs "in the moment" if you have a problem during a lesson.

One of the greatest things about virtual lessons is that you have the freedom to sample different instructors from around the world as well as from across the country. Many of these instructors boast impressive backgrounds and reputations, and their lessons are generally within a reasonable price range. Another advantage is that if you decide to switch instructors, doing so online is less awkward than doing so face to face.

The second challenge is getting the proper equipment and learning how to use it. For the technically unsavvy among us, this can be as challenging as figuring out how to harness a driving horse. You will probably need someone to record the video. Placing a camera on a fencepost or tripod won't capture much useful footage.

A better solution is a system that enables the camera to follow you and even zoom in and out as you ride around the ring. The prices and quality of the systems vary greatly. Some are very user-friendly, while others seemed designed only for the most "geekish" of geeks. If possible, try them out before you buy. There's a good chance that a local school's athletic department, a Little League team, or a golf pro at a local course has one. You'll also have a learning curve to understand how to upload or send the recordings. Most of the systems try to be easy to follow, but if you are challenged by checking your email, you'll need a tutor. If you can't find a friendly teenager who was born knowing these things, check with the community college that undoubtedly has computer courses, or look for online classes, most of which are free.

**Self-Directed Study**

If you have some experience and want to structure your own training program, you'll find plenty of material to choose from. There are as many online instructional videos as there are flies in the summer and more books than in a Barnes and Noble warehouse.

Look for clips from symposiums, conventions, or competitions. You'll find sessions by top trainers explaining dressage moves, measuring the distance to a jump, or timing of successful calf roping. These are gold because you are watching the best in their disciplines working with dedicated riders. While many videos feature advanced riders and instruction, you'll find many demonstrations with lower-level riders. Watch videos of championship rides and absorb the magic of the partnership. There is always something to learn, and if nothing else, it is great entertainment.

Take advantage of websites with vast libraries of videos from professionals, universities, veterinarians, and champion riders. Some are free, while others charge a subscription. Riding instruction is included in many of these collections. The expected subjects are well-represented, but every equine topic—designing a jump course, successful trailer loading, backing a trailer, even how to clean a horse's sheath—is found on one of these sites. So are interviews with top riders, documentaries about famous horses, and videos of Olympic competition.

New riders find illustrated books, e-books, and streaming videos covering the basics of riding exercises, workbooks to track your progress, "how to" for grooming, guides to tack and bits, groundwork exercises, and horse handling. These have thorough instructions and plenty of photos.

**Clinics**

Whenever a well-known or experienced instructor is within driving distance, attend the clinic, even if it is not in your preferred discipline or if you are not riding in the clinic yourself. Most clinics have riders at a variety of levels. You'll often see as many intermediate riders as upper-level and seasoned competitors. You will always learn something: a new technique for a common problem, a fresh way to approach your horse, a new angle to look at a situation. You'll start to develop an eye for good riding, and it is inspiring to watch someone and realize, "I can do that." If the clinician offers video training, this is an excellent way to "audition" her and decide if you want to ride with her program.

## Podcasts and Webinars

While not generally useful for teaching riding, podcasts and webinars are excellent sources for finding in-depth and professional information about horses. There are at least 50 podcasts that deal with horses in some way. You'll wear out your ears listening to interviews with riders and trainers, tips on grooming and horse care, reviews of new products, and advice on equine health. Webinars are often presented by state extension or agriculture departments or veterinary schools. Riding is rarely the subject. Instead, the professionals discuss topics like fly control, toxic plants in pastures, and deworming protocols. Most of these are free to download.

## Social Media

While social media is excellent for finding simpatico horsewomen, social media groups and chat rooms are not the best places to look for riding instruction or solutions to behavioral or medical issues. Every question generates a dozen or more answers and suggestions, which can be excellent but also erroneous and possibly dangerous. Most people offer well-meaning advice, but you do not know that person's experience, whether she understands the situation correctly, and if her answer is within the realm of realistic solutions. Even if the person offering advice is a professional, her advice is based on the interpretation of a written description or a video that may not have all of the pertinent information. There is at least one social media group that is dedicated to veterinary questions. Only veterinarians are allowed to comment. Overall, however, with health issues, the rule of thumb must always be, when in doubt, call the vet.

## Other Equine Areas of Interest

Several schools and equine organizations offer home study courses in areas other than riding. These generally focus on non-riding aspects of the horse world, like stable management, emergency preparedness, horse health and behavior, nutrition, and equine business management. The University of Guelph in Toronto is especially noted for its wide range of affordable home study courses. A few accredited colleges and universities offer online programs that lead to an associate degree or a non-credit certificate of completion.

# CHAPTER 3

# A Stable Environment: The Place, the People, and You

Entering the horse world can be very confusing. It's not a retail or business setting where most companies are similarly organized. In the horse world, each stable, riding school, and farm is unique.

Often there are as many different people in charge as there are varieties of grain at the feed store. There are dozens of variations of ownership, responsibilities, and operations. Each combination affects how the place operates. Those probably won't play a big role in your experience, but things are very fluid in the equestrian world. The people you work and ride with today might leave for a new opportunity or instructor next week.

For you, the general tone of the operation matters greatly. What is the "feel" of the place? Some women appreciate the exuberance and antics of child riders and enjoy riding at a stable with a kids' program. Others look at the stable as a peaceful oasis and want as much quiet and predictability as possible. Find out what's likely to be happening when you are most likely riding.

Are the boarders and students long-term clients? People stay where they are happy and feel they are getting their money's worth. Are the other people at the barn welcoming? Are they willing to show you around and answer questions? Most riders love to meet other horse people and proudly show off their stable. Do they share your interests and attitudes? Do you see yourself fitting in? You'll be spending a lot of your life at this place. You want to like the people as much as the horses.

The physical condition of the stable is important. It reflects the priorities of the owners and shows concern for safety, organization, and care of the horses. It is an important consideration in choosing where to ride.

## GOOD MANNERS MATTER

Going to the stable, breathing in the sweet scents of fresh hay and horsehair, and being a part of a community of horse lovers is one of the joys of life. You enjoy spending time at your oasis of comfort and security. When you ride, you forget that there is anything in the universe except the two of you, horse and rider, pal and partner. Ideally, you find a new family at the barn who shares your love of horses, who are equally eager to learn, and who actually enjoy mucking stalls and cleaning tack.

Well-run stables strive to create a good atmosphere. They encourage students and boarders to hang out. There may be a break room with a fridge and snacks, a pile of old horse magazines, an ancient sagging couch, and maybe a TV and collection of books and videos. Some barns organize pleasure rides and cookouts, and if people at the barn compete, there's encouragement from the rest of the riders, including those who don't show but who go to events to cheer on their friends.

Because stables are busy with people sharing space, times, facilities, and sometimes equipment, social niceties are important. In a perfect world, people would naturally display basic respect and courtesy, be tidy, leave other people's things alone, clean up after themselves and their horses, and treat everyone as they want

# Barn Amenities: "Must Haves" or "Bonus Points"?

➤ Is the barn clean and in good repair? An old barn may show its age, but it should still be sturdy. During any day, grooming kits will end up sitting on tack boxes and horses will track dirt and bits of hay into the aisle, but even a novice can tell if debris is routine daily clutter or chronic messiness.

➤ Are stalls clean? A pile or two of manure in a stall is normal when horses are inside during the day, but several piles that have been walked over or urine-soaked shavings are not good signs.

➤ Unless an obsessive-compulsive cleaner runs the barn, spider webs and dust will hang from the rafters, but that's usually because reaching them is almost impossible. You can accept them as part of the ambiance, but are they covering windows and stalls? What sort of soot is around the stall doors and storage areas?

➤ Is there a central spot where brooms, shovels, and muck buckets are kept, or are they scattered about?

➤ Are storage bins secure and the floor swept in the feed room? Is there a chart that shows the feed requirements for each horse? Are feed buckets and other supplies organized neatly?

➤ Is there a break room or hangout area? It isn't vital, but it's nice to have a place to chat instead of standing in the middle of the barn aisle. It could be a picnic table outside or an enclosed viewing area overlooking the arena. Some barns have rooms with small refrigerators and microwaves.

➤ Is there a notice board where people can leave messages and where important notices are posted? Things like scheduled dates for the dentist and farrier and information about upcoming rides, clinics, or shows. There should be a list of important numbers like the vet, farrier, and fire department hanging in a prominent place. If there is no landline, is there a strong cell signal?

➤ Is there an accessible fire extinguisher?

➤ Are there security cameras? Is the tack room secured during the day if no one is around and at night? A lock and security cameras deter theft and help with insurance claims if there is theft.

## AGELESS ADVICE

➤ Is the tack room organized with saddles and bridles on racks, or are things heaped on the floor? Saddles and bridles may be old, but are they clean and in good repair?

➤ Are the supplies neatly arranged at the wash stall? Is the hose coiled after use? Does the wash rack have hot water? It's not necessary but is very nice. (Extra points if there is a washer/dryer on premises and four-star ratings if there is a shower for humans.)

➤ Is there a toilet or at least a port-a-pot? Peeing in the stall may be a time-honored tradition, but at our age, we might have trouble getting back up if we have to squat.

➤ Playing radios is controversial. Often stables keep a radio playing for entertainment. Some people claim this desensitizes horses to noise. Others say that horses are prey animals and need to hear their natural environment and surroundings to feel safe.

➤ Are students responsible for bringing in, grooming, and tacking up their horses? That interaction is important in building a relationship and learning about horses and horse care. You want to ride where you handle your mount before and after the lesson. Is there someone in the barn who can help you if you need it?

➤ If the horses are kept in stalls, do they seem contented and relaxed? Do they pace, weave, or crib, which can be signs of poor management?

➤ If they are kept in a field, are they grazing contentedly? Do they seem to get along, or is there herd tension? Are they easy to catch and bring in? Are they easy to handle when coming in from the field?

➤ Are students required to wear safety helmets? Are adult riders wearing them? Are non-student riders wearing them? Most insurance companies require helmets for lessons for children, and many barns require that all riders wear helmets regardless of their age or experience. If helmets are optional and riders are not using them, that's a warning sign that rider safety may not be a high priority.

Many of these things are not requirements, and the more amenities a place offers, the more it will probably charge for lessons or board. You must decide which are vital and which are optional.

to be treated. Sadly, courtesy, common sense, and good manners don't always make their way to the stable. Given that we are probably older than many of the other people at the barn, our inherent maturity, seniority, and implied authority and experience can go a long way toward helping maintain a respectful atmosphere.

Many stables have a written set of rules that are often posted in the tack room or lounge. These include guidelines related to behavior toward other riders, instructors, vendors, and visitors; where and how equipment is stored; using other people's things; cleaning up muck; cleaning shared tack; interacting with other people's horses; parking; pets and kids; visitors; and safety procedures such as the use of helmets. Some stables include the rules in lesson or boarding agreements. Before accepting a new student or boarder, the stable manager reviews the rules and has the new boarder initial each of them. If the rules change, the boarder initials the new ones.

Rules—written or otherwise—are enforced strictly, occasionally, or not at all. Sometimes, those in charge don't want to risk an unfriendly confrontation. It's possible that the boarders who ignore the rules are friends of those in charge, or they make up such a significant portion of the stable's bottom line that the manager can't afford to make them angry and risk them leaving. No matter what others do, you should always act respectfully and with common sense and courtesy.

Even with clearly stated rules, there's a lot of give-and-take at a stable. No one likes conflict, and letting things slide occasionally is probably a good strategy for keeping everyone on good terms. Inevitably, sponges in the wash rack are shared, or someone grabs your horse's lead rope because it's more convenient at that moment for that situation. That's normal. But if you decide you're dealing with more "give" than "take," you should mention this.

Say politely but firmly that you don't mind lending things occasionally, but you appreciate being asked first and seeing borrowed items returned. Write your name on everything you own: brushes, spray bottles, shipping boots, hoof picks, and saddle pads. If the problem persists, invest in a lockable tack box. You may have to store things in your trailer or go through the hassle of keeping your tack in your car and toting it back and forth from home.

## GOSSIP

Few things can poison the atmosphere at a stable like nasty gossip.

Because horses and riders are usually empathic, we feel emotions and react more strongly than others. Horses draw out our emotions, which is why we are drawn to them when we need a personal release. That ability to expose and connect to our feelings has a downside, however.

Emotions create drama, and the equestrian world thrives on drama. But sadly, many stables house not only horses but also cats. Not the ones chasing mice, but catty women and men. At these places, you hear gossip, rumors, and innuendo about other riders, trainers, barn owners, their spouses, their personal lives, and businesses, usually in juicy detail. It's a toss-up as to how much of it is accurate.

Few of us are immune to the lure of gossip. Watching snarky reality shows is a guilty pleasure for many of us. In real life, it is tempting to join in, especially if you want to be accepted by a group or if you also don't particularly like the target of the gossip.

To be sure, most chatter is just information. As humans, we are hard-wired to share information about ourselves and others. It has helped us survive as a species ("Yo, Trog, watch out for that saber-toothed tiger creeping up behind you!") and to develop friendships and communities. Trading news is a normal part of human curiosity, especially when it concerns people we know. "Shooting the breeze" is not necessarily harmful. Whether it crosses the line from chatter to nasty gossip depends on the intent of those sharing the news, whether or not it is true, and how it is shared.

The repercussions are never healthy. "Alternative facts," even when disproved, never die, and usually spread far beyond the farm's fence line. If it goes unchecked, barn gossip creates an atmosphere that sucks the joy out of riding.

Ideally, those who run the stable do not tolerate barn drama and call out the gossips as soon as they learn of it. It's in their interest to keep the atmosphere at the stable upbeat. They need boarders and students bringing in fees to pay their bills. Word spreads quickly about unpleasant stables with unpleasant riders. Some barns incorporate "No gossip, no drama" into their posted barn rules.

If you are in a gossip-laden situation, minimize your exposure. Be cordial but find something else to do when the cat-fest starts. Rearrange your tack, take your horse out to hand-graze, watch a lesson. If you are pulled into the conversation, don't participate. One of the greatest comments for many situations is, "How interesting." That's it. Nothing else. Just, "How interesting," and go back to what you were doing. Another is to turn the talk into a joke: "Honey, I have so much drama in my life that I don't have time for anyone else's."

There are some situations that you cannot ignore or learn to live with. In these situations, you must take it to the management. If more than one person fills that role, you might meet with all of them.

You must act if you see kids being bullied, either by other kids or worse, by adults. Pre-teen and teenaged girls are particularly vulnerable to the pettiness that seems to be a rite of passage in some groups. If you feel comfortable asking the target, find out if this treatment is routine and if the adults in her life know about it. If nothing else, mention the bullying to the people in charge. They should want to weed out that sort of behavior.

Sadly, cases of sexual abuse have darkened the equestrian world as they have with other sports. In response to the scandals involving sexual abuse of gymnasts, swimmers, equestrians, and competitors in other sports, the US Center for SafeSport created an online training and education program. The course teaches the often subtle signs of actual and potential abuse. If you are a dues-paying member of a national equestrian organization, you must complete the program in order to compete in any licensed or sponsored show. If you are not a member but want to become educated about the subject, you can take the training for a nominal fee. It takes only a few hours that you can spread out over several days. It is well-presented, interesting, and informative. It is an eye-opening experience for those of us who come from a generation where such things were thought unimaginable.

You must act if you suspect that a child is being physically or sexually abused. If the facility has several people in management positions, you must speak to the highest-ranking person. Do not discuss your suspicions with others at the barn, only the management.

Other reasons for talking with management include a situation that is dangerous to horses or riders. This is particularly important at barns where the owner or manager is off the property more than onsite and supervising. Such situations can involve feeding and nutrition, herd dynamics, maintenance of fencing and buildings, and rodent infestation.

## SWITCHING BARNS OR MOVING ON

There are many reasons for moving barns. Maybe you and your trainer have progressed as far as you can together. Maybe your schedules no longer mesh, and you can't find a convenient lesson time. Maybe you want to try a different discipline. Maybe your instructor specializes in beginners, and you've moved beyond that. Maybe teaching was a side gig for your instructor, and she's found a full-time job. Maybe you've found a barn that's more convenient or cheaper.

The search for a new barn is much like your original search. However, now that you have more contacts in the local horse world, it might be easier. The process is still the same: get some names, visit the farms, talk to the manager, the owners, the instructor, the other students and boarders. If there are no hard feelings, let the people at your current stable know that you are looking around and why. It is often difficult to tell the current barn instructor/owner/manager that you are leaving. That's particularly true if you like everyone, but other factors outweigh you staying. You want to leave on good terms. If there are no overriding negative reasons for your going, the management should be professional and understanding.

Expect the people at the prospective new barns to ask why you want to move. They will naturally be curious. If nothing else, they want to see if you might be a nightmare boarder or student who'll bring angst and headaches along with tack and a grooming kit.

If negative rumors are circulating about your current barn, you will hear them. Stay non-committal. Don't spread any stories. Don't make negative comments, no matter how deliciously tempting it is. Not about the other riders or boarders; not about the managers or instructors, their abilities, or their personal lives; not about the horses; not about the condition of the barn. Don't burn any bridges. It will come back to haunt you. Forget "six degrees of separation." The horse world is smaller than that.

When you find a new stable, immediately tell the management of your current barn. That is simple professional courtesy. This must be done face to face, not via e-mail, phone call, or messaging. Do not tell other people at the barn that you are leaving until management knows. It is rude for them to hear it second-hand.

It is customary to give 30 days' notice of ending a boarding or lesson contract. That gives the barn and instructor a chance to find someone to fill your spot. You should pay the final 30 days' board or the completion of your student contract unless they offer to pro-rate it. While an amicable departure usually goes smoothly, be ready to leave immediately if asked to do so. The management may have a waiting list for boarding or teaching. They may also want you to leave immediately to prevent any awkwardness between them, you, and the rest of the people at the barn.

If you are leaving under less-than-pleasant circumstances, anticipate an angry reaction. When the departure conversation turns unpleasant, stay calm and do not argue back. Just like with a friendly parting, pay the 30 days' board or the completion of any lesson contract. You might be ordered to leave immediately, so have things set up at your new barn. That's especially important if you are moving a horse. Be ready to pack out your tack and other belongings right away and have transportation to move your horse if you do not have a trailer. If you are allowed to stay but worry about your horse's safety, your possessions, or yourself, move immediately, even if you lose the 30 days' board. The financial hit is worth the peace of mind.

CHAPTER 4

# What to Wear:
# Equine Fashionistas

You can't be a rider without proper riding clothes. The empty closet space created when you donated your work clothes to charity will soon be filled with your new wardrobe of things to wear around the stable.

An entire world of equine fashion statements waits to tempt you. You'll flip through catalogs and browse websites showing stylish, spotlessly clean ensembles worn by svelte lovelies with perfect hair and nails who never stood near a horse before the photoshoot, much less mucked stalls or picked hay out of their bras.

Age is no factor in finding riding clothes. What you buy and what you wear are decided by your sense of style and the limit of your credit card. You can be practical and stick with serviceable t-shirts and jeans, or indulge yourself with logoed blouses and designer breeches. Bling is in, so celebrate the brightness of your new life with a bit of glitter and shine. In warm weather or sunny locations, try shirts with vented backs for breathability, sunblock technology, wick-away cloth, and fabric impregnated with insect repellant. Cold weather brings out winter layers of fleece and Thinsulate™. There are jackets for cool weather, jackets for rainy weather, and jackets for snowy weather;

gloves for every discipline and chore; boots for daily riding, dress boots for showing, paddock boots, all-purpose shoes, muckers, and Wellies; jeans, riding denims, and riding pants; breeches in traditional brown and beige, but also bright colors and patterns. Announce your independence from stereotypes about our age group by wearing t-shirts with clever sayings like, "Never underestimate an old woman who rides."

You will, of course, be sensible about the whole thing and buy only what you absolutely need. You will not give in to the temptation to commit your credit card number to memory in order to save time while ordering online.

## YOUR DAILY RIDING WARDROBE

The basic riding kit for English riders is a helmet, boots, shirt, gloves, and breeches. If you show, you'll need a tailored shirt, and add a jacket and tie or stock collar, depending on your discipline. Western riders need a helmet, boots, shirt, and jeans. For Western shows, competitors turn out in colorful blouses, dress hats, and chaps.

For most of us, online shopping is probably our best bet. Even if you live near a retail store that carries riding wear, the inventory is usually fairly limited. Online you'll find everything you need, want, and desire. When drawing up your shopping list, you'll notice that several sites often have the same product, but at different prices. Don't default to the lowest price. A retailer with a lower list price than its competitors might charge a higher shipping fee. Check return policies. Many retailers require you to pay return shipping or charge a return or restocking fee.

## HEADGEAR

Wearing a hard hat is an essential safety precaution. Most riding schools and instructors require helmets. Even if you are in a state with an "inherent risk" (ride at your own risk) law, if you fall and suffer any kind of head trauma, the personal injury lawyers will swarm around the instructor and the facility like flies at a manure pile. While you may not want to sue, it is likely your insurance company will go after whomever it can, in order to get its money back.

Your helmet must be approved by ASTM/SEI. These are international organizations that set safety standards for such equipment. New helmets that incorporate MIPS (Multi-directional Impact Protection System) technology, which mimics your brain's own protection system, are also becoming available. (More details on the standards and testing are found in the "Safety" section—see p. 91.)

There is no need to buy a $500 show helmet with Swarovski crystals for daily wear. Schooling helmets that cost one-quarter to one-half that will serve the purpose. All helmets have similar designs but look different on each person. A helmet that sits nicely and flatters one woman's head can look like a mushroom perched on top of the ears on another. Many brands offer helmets in colors or trendy designs. In general, if you plan to show, the helmet should be black, brown, or dark navy blue, especially at larger or recognized shows. Schooling shows and informal contests are more welcoming to different colors, although brightly patterned helmets tend to be frowned upon. (Check with the show manager if you are uncertain. You can buy fabric covers in dark colors to cover that pink or purple helmet in the show ring.)

Design and color aside, the only thing that matters is the fit. The staff at your l ocal tack shop can fit yours properly. There are also good visual tutorials online. The helmet should be snug enough that after you fasten the chin strap, it stays in place when you nod your head vigorously and turn from side to side. Never ride without fastening the chin strap. Otherwise, when you fall, the first thing that goes flying through the air is your helmet. (Links to videos on proper helmet fit can be found at www.ridersofacertainage.com.)

Several manufacturers sell Western helmets. That's something of a misnomer. They are the traditional English helmets but are tan with leather or suede inserts for a more Western look. The only traditional-styled Western hat approved by ASTM/SEI is the RideSafe Western hat from Resistol.

The other Western option is the HellHat. Invented by Mark and Karen Plumlee, following a fall in which Karen fractured her skull, it's a DIY hybrid of a helmet and a traditional Western hat. The crown of the Western hat is cut out, and the helmet inserted in its place. The two pieces are glued together to create a Western-looking safety helmet. Some companies sell brims that attach to the helmet with elastic or Velcro. Be aware that manufacturers invalidate the warranty on helmets if they are modified in any way, including inserting them into the HellHat design.

Helmets must be replaced every five years, regardless of whether you've fallen. That is because materials deteriorate over time. No matter how lightly your head hits the ground, the helmet must be replaced. Some manufacturers ask you to return the helmet so they can examine it and continually improve the design. Some will replace the helmet; others might give a discount for a new one.

## FOOTWEAR

Except for your helmet, what's on your feet is even more important than what's on your body. Proper footwear is vital no matter what you are doing with or around your horse or barn. Running shoes, trainers, and slip-on espadrilles are non-starters in the saddle. You need ankle support and a solid sole and heel. Never wear open-toed shoes, flip-flops, or sandals at the barn, even when you are not riding. Aside from the discomfort of getting dirt, hay, and horse poop between your toes, imagine what happens when a 1,000-pound horse steps on your bare foot.

Western riders have it easy. Cowboy boots are the standard. The classic style with a pointed toe can be very uncomfortable if you have toe or foot conditions that are aggravated in tight spaces. Look for boots with a box toe design. Even if the classic fit is comfortable, consider that your feet will swell on long rides, and a roomier toe might be a better choice. Pay attention to the height of the heel. If you have back or knee issues, a higher heel will be fine in a saddle but can cause discomfort when walking around.

It's a bit more complicated for English riders. Depending on what you are doing, choose between paddock boots, all-purpose shoes, and tall boots. Muck boots and Wellies are suitable for doing barn chores, but not for riding.

Some riders adhere to the philosophy that you should practice and train in the same footwear you will use when you show, so they wear tall boots during lessons. Others wear paddock boots, sometimes with chaps or half-chaps, for lessons and daily barn activities and save their good boots for shows. Paddock boots come up to just above your ankle. There are zip-up, lace-up, and pull-on versions. They are made of leather or a weatherproof synthetic. You want them to be snug around the ankle but still allow for flexibility. Which one you choose is a personal preference; they make no difference in your riding.

An option for both Western and English riders is the all-purpose "terrain boot." The styling is similar to a trail or hiking shoe, but the sole and heel are designed for riding. These shoes are a good option for riders looking for a wider toe and a flatter heel.

Whatever you ride, buy the best quality footwear you can afford and take care of it. Treat the shoes or boots with leather conditioner when you buy them, keep them clean, and they will last for years.

## GLOVES

Although people often don't think of gloves as essential riding wear, they are as important as any other piece of a rider's clothing. Ranch hands and riders competing in barrel racing, reining, and roping need durable gloves to protect their hands from the rigors of those activities. Trainers appreciate the extra grip on reins when working with young and rambunctious horses. Endurance and hunter/jumper riders need those same benefits. Equitation and dressage riders find that gloves allow them to deliver more finesse as they seek "softness" in their communication between horse and rider. Many trail riders do not routinely use gloves but often benefit from the protection they give in summer from bug bites and sunburn.

When buying gloves, consider use and durability. Ranch gloves are generally made of heavy leather, while some gloves for dressage are as thin as a second skin.

Many riders have more gloves than Dolly Parton has wigs. There are gloves with leather or silicon on the fingers and palms to improve grip, with backs made of crocheted yarn for breathability in hot weather or lined with fleece or Thinsulate™ for winter wear. Show gloves may have sequins or other bling around the wrist. Aside from dressage, which requires white gloves in competition, what you wear is an entirely personal choice.

Gloves come in inches or international sizing. To find your size, measure your hand's girth without the thumb, then use the manufacturer's sizing chart. They should be snug but allow for complete movement of your fingers, thumb, and wrist.

## JEANS AND BREECHES

Here again, Western riders get a break. Jeans are what Western riders wear. Most manufacturers have at least one line of jeans designed specifically for horseback riders. Some are cut higher in the back, have stretch fabric for riding comfort, no-gap waistbands, flat seams, no inseam, and mid-rise to natural waistbands for those of us who are long past the low-cut stage of life.

Some riders wear chaps or chinks, which are leather leggings that wrap around your lower leg. These give a better grip and protect your legs when on trail rides. Since you wear chaps when you show, you don't need to have a special pair of jeans set aside for the show ring, although most competitors opt to buy show pants, which often have a more flattering fit.

For English riders, breeches are high on the shopping list. Riding in jeans might work for the first few lessons, but the fabric moves, the seams are in the wrong place, and it is hard to keep your legs in the proper position. Half-chaps that wrap around your lower leg solve some of these problems, but breeches provide better contact and stability. There are as many styles, colors, and patterns of breeches as there are ribbons at a horse show. What matters is the fit. Breeches should be snug but allow you to move, stretch, and sit comfortably. There is no standard as to sizing. One brand's size 14 is another's 10. The general S, M, L, XL are vague guidelines. "Standard" waistline can mean it sits at your hips or comes dangerously close to giving you plumber's butt. You need to try them on.

Breeches are either "knee patch" or "full seat." This refers to patches made of suede, leather, silicone, or some synthetic material on the leg of the breeches. They help stabilize your leg and derrière. A knee patch is on the inside of the leg from the knee to partway down the leg. Full seat patches run from the knee to cover the entire seat of the breeches. Knee patch breeches are preferred by jumper and hunter riders since they do not sit very often. Breeches are made of cotton blends, polyester, and other breathable, stretchable fabrics. Recognizing that most of us lost our flat tummies around menopause and that breeches are unforgiving in hiding our figures, some brands offer breeches with control panels.

Traditionally breeches were beige, black, tan, and gray. Occasionally, some rebellious rider would show up wearing retro rust-colored breeches. But, overall, English riding fashion was the sartorial equivalent to wearing a corset. That's changing. For lessons, there are no rules. Wear whatever is comfortable.

## CLOTHING FOR COMPETITION

Each discipline has its own requirements when it comes to show clothes. They are likely to be a spin on your everyday lesson and barn wear. If you do decide to compete, talk to your instructor, riding friends, and salespeople at the local tack shop about what you absolutely need and what can serve you well in both worlds. If splurging is on the menu, they can direct you toward all the prettiest, shiniest things, too.

# PART TWO

# FITNESS AND THE RIDER OF A CERTAIN AGE

# CHAPTER 5

# Easing into the Saddle: Knowing What You Can Do

As riders, we expect our horses to be physically fit and able to do what we ask with power and ease. We shouldn't ask any less of ourselves.

Whether we hop into the saddle for a casual outing or are serious competitors, all riders require certain physical abilities. We need to move fluidly with our horses, relax our joints, and use subtle signals to communicate. We need the balance and flexibility of a gymnast, the timing and coordination of a diver, and the stamina of a marathon runner. There is no other athletic pursuit that requires so many elements.

For younger riders, this is not a problem. The relative lack of mileage on their bodies leaves them able to maintain a demanding riding regimen and meet those physical needs with aplomb.

For the rest of us? While our years have graced us with wisdom and experience, we've also collected a host of physical issues that the youngsters who hop onto their 16.2 Warmbloods without a mounting block can't imagine. Osteoarthritis, heart disease, tight ligaments, loose urinary muscles, and damage from old injuries and operations are just a few of the complaints.

There are also some age-related problems that are not as immediately recognizable. Muscle atrophy is one. We lose about one-half pound of muscle every year after age 25; we also grow shorter as our spines start to compress from general aging, not to mention damage from years of poor posture. The neuro-muscular connection slows, affecting reaction time, balance, and recall (aka those "senior moments" I mentioned earlier in the book). Bones start to lose density and do not rebuild as quickly if broken. We've lost flexibility, which can make following the movement of our horses a tense and uncomfortable experience. A strong, stable core is the most important thing for staying secure in the saddle and being able to give clear aids to your horse, but between physical changes thanks to menopause, weak muscles from childbirth, and inattention to proper exercise and eating habits, our abdominal muscles are often weak.

On the other hand, active seniors generally have lower blood pressure, better heart health, and fewer cases of diabetes. We benefit from the exercise, socialization, and the restorative effects of being outside. Riders have higher levels of serotonin, which regulates sleep, appetite, moods, and sex drive. Not to mention the tonic of maintaining a sense of independence and purpose at a time when society often seems to channel us to passive activity and dependent status.

Starting to ride at any age means a change in your physical routine. For younger women, the most they'll complain about is the discovery of muscles they didn't know they had. For us, however, age-related issues require a more thorough assessment of where we are and what we can do.

You may have been a hell-bent-for-leather bareback riding daredevil when you were a kid, but your once-limber joints and flexible muscles are not as youthfully cooperative as they once were. You can't pick up riding from where you stopped years ago.

Before you get into the saddle, either as a returning rider or a new one, you need to honestly assess your physical condition and identify the obvious and potential problems. A caveat here to suggest that you visit your primary care physician and give her a heads-up on your plans. Don't be surprised if you get a lecture about how you are "too old for that kind of foolishness." Your doctor has legitimate concerns. We are more fragile than her younger patients. In addition to the general changes in our bodies from age, after-effects from operations and illnesses can limit our abilities, and she must point them out.

You might be tempted to politely point out that Queen Elizabeth II, well into her nineties, rides almost daily; that safety vests and protective headgear are routinely used; and that unless you are racing, jumping, or competing in rodeos, riding isn't much more dangerous than sitting on the coin-operated horses in the lobby at Walmart.

However, that's not the case. Studies show that horseback riding is more dangerous than football, rugby, or skiing. Horseback riding sees more hospitalizations than more extreme activities like motorcycle racing.

Falls are responsible for most of those injuries. One study in New Zealand shows that there is one fall for every 100 hundred hours of leisure riding. But nearly 30 percent of injuries happen on the ground while tacking up, grooming, feeding, getting kicked, stepped on, or bitten.

None of the studies have statistics about our age group. They are all either sport-specific, like eventing, or come from the under-30 age group. Statistics on the rate and severity of injuries for us do not exist.

As older adults, our "ideal" fitness can't be pigeonholed. The groups that assess fitness and design programs for the general public are still trying to determine how far older adults can go physically. Their research focuses on biking, swimming, and aerobics. They haven't begun to figure out what's best for crazy ladies who climb onto the back of a 1,200-pound animal and trot around for fun.

The equestrian world itself has no clear idea of our capabilities. For example, The Equestrian Medical Association, the group that supplies EMTs and medics at major horse shows, has a fitness assessment. However, it is for the under-30s, so it is not much use to us. Equestrian Canada has long-term development guidelines that call for cross-training three to four times a week for 60 to 90 minutes each time. Non-equestrian fitness programs suggest similar schedules for active adults.

Those numbers are targets for younger people. If you haven't been working out regularly or if you have physical issues, it may take weeks, if not months, to safely and comfortably reach that goal, if ever. Just as it takes time to condition your horse, you need time to build an effective program for yourself, particularly if the most exercise you've had in years is walking your dog, strolling to the office break room, or working in your flower garden. The intensity of the fitness schedule and mix of elements depends on your starting point and a realistic assessment of your condition and abilities. There are as many different approaches to developing a fitness routine as there are different riding breeches. And just like the breeches, there is no such thing as "one size fits all."

If you haven't already, you will meet people who roll their eyes and tell you, "Riding isn't exercise. The horse does all the work." Not so, according to Texas A&M, which conducted a study of how many calories riders burn in an hour. The researchers found that a 160-pound adult riding for two hours a week burns about 1,300 calories. That's the same as a brisk, one-hour walk five days a week. One FitBit user discovered that her one-hour English riding lesson burns as many calories as her hour-long spin class. If much of that lesson is spent posting, that equals a lot of crunches and workouts on the Stairmaster.

But wait! There's more! The regular barn chores are the real fat-burners. Loading and stacking hay bales comes in at 700 calories per hour (not to mention giving you a terrific upper-body workout). Mucking stalls and grooming clock in at around 500 calories an hour, depending on how many stalls need tending and how much mud is caked onto your horse. In comparison, players in a game of pickup basketball burn off a mere 340 calories an hour.

## The Equestrian Workout

Kentucky Performance Products developed this delightful chart that estimates how many calories per hour a 150-pound person burns in an hour riding and completing barn chores.

| ACTIVITIES AROUND THE BARN | CALORIES PER HOUR |
| --- | --- |
| Clean Stalls | 550 |
| Feed Horses | 306 |
| Groom | 525 |
| Walk in Field | 335 |
| Drive Tractor | 150 |
| Paint Fences | 140 |
| Shovel Snow | 450 |
| Mow Lawn | 457 |

| RIDING A HORSE | CALORIES PER HOUR |
| --- | --- |
| At the Halt | 78 |
| Walk | 168 |
| Post Trot | 420 |
| Sitting Trot | 450 |
| Canter | 514 |
| Gallop | 558 |
| Jogging Slowly After a Loose Horse | 550 |

Information courtesy of Kentucky Performance Products (kppusa.com).

Some of us already have a fitness regime and just need to tweak it for riding. Others know enough about physical training to design their own program. Some people use fitness apps to record their workouts and stay motivated. Others sign up for an online exercise program.

A few dedicated souls have the discipline to work out regularly without outside motivation. They watch videos or follow outlines in exercise books, some of which are specifically for equestrians. The rest of us need encouragement. Depending on the quality of your maternal instincts or the stability of your personal relationships, a nagging child or spouse might also keep you working out. Seek out an accountability buddy, maybe someone else at the stable, who will work out with you. Some social media groups, specifically for horseback riders, act as virtual accountability buddies.

CHAPTER 6

# Getting Fit:
# Training, Trainers, and Therapies

**FINDING A TRAINER**

If you don't know your pecs from your hamstrings, consider working with a personal trainer. Even if you understand exercise and have the motivation to work out on your own, booking a few sessions with a trainer helps you pinpoint the best exercises for your specific needs and how to perform them correctly. That's critical, because if you have bad form, you are not only working the muscles incorrectly, but you also stand a chance of injuring yourself.

It's a big plus if the trainer rides. Most do not, however, and they think that you need powerful arms and legs so that you can pull your horse's head with your biceps and shoulders and kick his ribs with your heels. They need to understand that you need deep core strength—not the muscles that give you six-pack abs, but the deep internal core muscles that provide you with center strength for stabilization and proper posture. Think in terms of the poise and balance of ice skaters and gymnasts. With that as a basis, you can work on flexibility so you can move more easily with your horse and cardiovascular exercises for stamina.

In choosing a trainer, find out her certifications. There are dozens of associations that certify trainers in over 1,500 areas. Some of those are very specific—trainers for cheerleaders, dance and hip-hop, golf, or water aerobics, for example. There is no special certification for equestrian training, unfortunately. Some associations have stringent requirements for education, training, testing, and continuing education in order to maintain certification. Others require little more than a weekend course, an open-book test, and a check that clears the bank.

Even if a trainer is certified by a respected association, it doesn't always follow that she is a good match for older clients. When you meet, let her know what you are doing and what your physical issues are. Like riding instructors, personal trainers need to know your situation to adjust their training accordingly. Many trainers are not used to working with our limitations. Most of the people at the gym are younger, more supple, and better able to push themselves. With the best of intentions, some trainers' ideas of easy workouts and slow-building strength and stamina exercises are with the mindset of working with someone with less mileage on them.

Don't feel self-conscious about what people at the gym think of your physical condition. Very few of them will notice or judge you. They have their own concerns. Feel free to wear baggy sweatpants and oversized T-shirts if they make you feel more comfortable. Remember, someday those Spandex-clad honeys will also have varicose veins and will look upon you as a role model.

## AT-HOME PERSONAL TRAINING

A growing segment of personal trainers works with clients at their homes. In some cases, they are trainers who meet most clients at a gym but who also make house calls. For others, their practice is entirely on the road. Still others have a gym at their home, and clients travel to them. Depending on the trainer, you might need

# Trainer Credentials

The most respected associations that certify personal trainers, in alphabetical order, are:

➤ ACSM: American College of Sports Medicine

➤ ACE: American Council on Exercise

➤ AFPA: American Fitness Professionals Association

➤ ASFA: American Sports and Fitness Association

➤ IFPA: International Fitness Professional Association

➤ ISSA: International Sports Science Association

➤ NASM: National Academy of Sports Medicine

➤ NFPT: National Federation of Professional Trainers

➤ NSCA: National Strength and Conditioning Association

When a personal trainer has completed training by one of these organizations, you can be confident that she is competent and up to date with the latest fitness training methods, trends, and research.

All these associations offer basic "personal training" certifications. In addition, each has other certifications that require additional coursework and testing. IFPA, for instance, has over 60 specialized certifications. These are as esoteric as "Exercise Endocrinology Specialist" and as practical as "Functional Aging Specialist." Almost all the associations have some program for working with seniors. However, most of those are designed for more sedentary and less active adults.

to own basic equipment like weights, exercise balls, resistance bands, and machines like a treadmill, elliptical, or stationary bike. Other trainers design programs that don't require machines and bring the gear they need with them. With the advent of video conferencing, some trainers are experimenting with teaching remotely. The advantages to at-home training: the sessions are part of your regular schedule, you avoid the hassle of getting to a gym, and you can't concoct a convenient reason to miss a workout. On the downside, such personal attention often comes with a higher price tag than working with a trainer at a gym.

## ONLINE TRAINING

This option works if you can't find a personal trainer you like or if your schedule or location makes working with a trainer or getting to a gym impossible.

The possibilities for individual online personal fitness training are overwhelming. A general search for "online fitness training" results in dozens of hits, each promising to connect you with a trainer who will take you to a level of fitness and health that most mere mortals only dream of. All of them share similar elements: personalized programs with goal setting, workout routines to build strength and flexibility, motivation and workout tips, advice on nutrition, and regular consultations to monitor your progress. Some of the programs are open-ended, while others are structured courses that run anywhere from 6 to 12 weeks. Only a handful of the programs target older participants. These feature low-impact exercises that focus on general fitness, flexibility, and balance. Most of the others are designed for serious athletes with ambitious goals, like bodybuilding or competing in triathlons, or people looking for high-impact, strenuous fitness routines.

Several online programs specifically target equestrians. These are personal training programs or daily workouts developed by trainers who are also riders or programs created by a rider and fitness professional working together. As with the

**AGELESS ADVICE**

## *Good Trainer Checklist*

A good trainer appreciates what you can handle and will design a program that's appropriate.

➤ She will know you need more time to develop or relearn muscle memory, safely increase muscle strength, improve balance, and build stamina.

➤ She should explain what she is doing and why it will help you.

➤ She should be able to adapt the program to adjust to your physical needs and limitations.

➤ She should invite questions from you about the exercises and overall fitness plan.

➤ She should give you a rough timeline for your progress.

➤ She should advise you on what you should do when you are working on your own.

On your part, you must let your trainer know if you are struggling, both during a session and after, particularly if you are hurting with more than the expected mild ache from working muscles.

If the trainer doesn't adapt to your needs, keep looking.

more general programs, the services and support vary, as do the costs. The advantage of these personal equine-centric courses is that you can tailor the program to include your physical abilities and riding goals.

As a result of the COVID-19 quarantine, the popularity of online group-training classes skyrocketed and continues to attract a strong following. Many require the purchase of an interactive treadmill, exercise bike, or elliptical machine. The purchase includes an app and membership (see p. 67) that allows you to connect with classes that create a sense of virtual community. Depending on the company, there are both live and archived classes in weight training, yoga, stretching, walking, cardio workouts, and Pilates.

## APPS

Apps are another way to find and use exercise routines, fitness advice, and nutritional support. Downloaded onto your device, they provide the convenience and luxury of opening them and working out wherever and whenever you please. You want to find user-friendly apps simple enough for beginners but that have enough variety and sophistication to adapt as your fitness level improves.

Some apps provide little more than a few exercises and a way to track your workouts. Others are amazingly detailed and include exercises, videos, animations, and live-action clips demonstrating how to perform an exercise. Some offer audio coaching, encourage goal-setting, and include charts to evaluate your progress.

Decide what you want the app to do: suggest exercises, track workouts, provide nutrition advice, link to a "buddies" network, offer online videos—whatever you want, there's an app with that. Then take off your boots, fix a cup of tea, prop up your feet, put on your reading glasses, and start scrolling through the links. Find a few that are intriguing, download them, and play with each one for a few weeks to find out which features are most helpful to you and which are useless. If an app seems lacking, move on to another. You don't have to worry about running out of apps to try.

## DIY WITH BOOKS AND VIDEOS

If you want to research and develop your own fitness routine, you might start with the many books that outline fitness programs for riders. In addition to showing exercises, the books give a lot of background about getting fit, how to adapt your current physical condition to your riding, and what to expect as you work out. As with other resources, few of these specifically address the needs of older riders, so you must assess your abilities and adjust as necessary. Some books have pre-designed fitness routines, while others target specific areas, like strengthening your core or maintaining a healthy back. While not written for equestrians, there are hundreds of books and videos that show you how to develop a strong core through floor exercises and by using balance balls and resistance bands.

Fitness articles found in horse-focused magazines include exercises and other health tips. You'll find a lot of overlapping advice and similar exercises for core strength, flexibility, and balance, which gives you an idea of your focus when planning your personal program.

While riding has some unique fitness needs that the equine-specific instruction can address, most of the toning you need is met by general workouts. "Beginner" cardio or "easy" Pilates workouts can be taxing, even when you opt for the low-intensity versions of an exercise. This is particularly true of workouts that combine both standing exercises and floor work. We're not as nimble as we once were, as routines that involve dropping to the floor then scrambling back to our feet remind us. Some "senior" routines are very low impact and are performed while sitting, which are usually too easy for us. But there are also "seniors" videos with Zumba, cardio, and strength training with light weights, power walking in place, and even belly dancing and ballroom dancing. (Don't laugh. Belly dancing loosens up your hips and lower back, while ballroom dancing is excellent for balance and coordination.)

Sample workouts in many areas, from meditation and yoga, to HIITS (high-intensity interval training) and cardio, to strength training and power walking. Then cobble together a "playlist" that includes equestrian, cardio, stretching, and strength training videos to create your own personalized, custom workouts. You can keep adding and changing the material, which helps you stay motivated.

## FITNESS TRACKERS

In some circles, Fitbit and its cousins are almost ubiquitous, with devotees monitoring their heart rates, counting their steps, and learning how well they sleep at night. Some models allow you to program your activities and count the calories you burn while doing daily chores and exercises. These can be adjuncts to a workout but are not much good for developing one.

Initially, fitness trackers did little more than count how many steps you walked each day and your heart rate. Now, they are sophisticated to the point of storing past workouts, synching with fitness buddies, sounding alarms if you've been idle for too long, using a "sunshine monitor" to detect UV ray exposure, tracking your walking route via GPS, and monitoring female health. (These primarily monitor menstrual cycles, although they can be somewhat helpful in tracking perimenopausal symptoms.)

The "calorie counting mode" for fitness trackers is geared toward interpreting movements that are consistent with walking or running, with some adjustments for swimming. The industry standard for those calculations is for reasonably fit, thirtyish-year-old males, although that bias is being corrected. Trackers that include "horseback riding" in their calorie-burning database can be misleading. The default hourly burn for most of them seems to be for quiet trail riding. If you are trotting or cantering, many of them give you a reading for jogging or running or completely shut down and give no reading at all.

With dozens of fitness trackers available, what you choose to buy, if you decide to use one at all, depends on the features. For seniors, there are a few features that are particularly important. Your activity—often translated into how many steps you take—is one. That's become the 10,000 steps per day benchmark, which translates roughly into 5 miles. Decide if that's a realistic starting point or a longer-term goal. For those of us busy with barn chores or chasing an uncatchable horse, we probably hit 10,000 steps before breakfast. Others need all day to hit that number or several weeks of slowly increasing activity to get there.

Heart rate is also important. Many charts provide the range of resting and working heart rates based on age. Learn what is normal for you and the level of activity needed to safely increase it and bring it back to the normal resting rate.

Monitoring your sleep sounds trivial, but it is important for seniors. Most people in our age group do not get enough good-quality sleep. Sleep deprivation is linked to heart disease, diabetes, weight gain, and a higher rate of breast cancer.

## BODYWORKS: THERAPIES FOR BALANCE AND STRENGTH

As we age, maintaining our mobility and stamina becomes a challenge. Even without major trauma to our system, decades of normal wear and tear, poor posture, and bad habits skew our bodies in ways that accelerate aging overall, not just make it less comfortable to ride. There are several practices and therapies that improve our physical condition. Pilates, yoga, chiropractic, and somatics are excellent additions to a well-rounded fitness plan. They make us more aware of our bodies and how we move. By strengthening our muscles and correcting poor alignment, they improve our posture and balance. As a result, we are more in control of our bodies both in and out of the saddle.

### Pilates

Pilates is perhaps the best way to develop the deep inner core muscles for a well-balanced body. It was developed after WWI by Joseph Pilates, who called it "Contrology." Using a combination of exercises and machines with resistance cables and springs, it develops strength, flexibility, and coordination of the all-important core, plus abs, back, shoulders, and hips. As an additional benefit, it strengthens the muscles of the pelvic floor, which helps ward off or correct urinary incontinence.

AGELESS ADVICE

## Important Fitness Tracker Features

On the technical side, the most important considerations in a fitness tracker, particularly if you are not gadget-savvy, are:

➤ **Display screen:** Is it large enough to read the numbers and other information easily? Are touch-screen controls clearly visible and large enough to be tapped without accidentally keying another control?

➤ **Ease of use:** Are the instructions simple and straightforward? Is there a physical instruction manual, or are the directions only online? Can you shift from one mode to another with one touch?

➤ **Durability:** Can it be worn in the shower or the pool? Will the screen and functions survive being dropped?

➤ **Battery life:** How long can it operate between recharges? Three days is the minimum recommendation. If it is battery-powered, six months to a year is recommended.

➤ **Privacy:** Some trackers, particularly those with a broader range of interactive features, require a smartphone or Bluetooth link. This might compromise personal privacy.

Pilates is a beneficial part of a riding program. There are online Pilates programs designed specifically for equestrians that are worth exploring. However, Pilates requires great concentration and focuses on very small movements and very strict control to do the movements correctly. If possible, go to a Pilates studio and work with a certified instructor one on one, or in a small class. Videos, books, and most large classes at gyms are often hard to follow and fail to provide the most effective feedback.

## Yoga

Perhaps the most well-known of the gentler forms of exercise, yoga is popular for its emphasis on stretching and balance. Because there are so many positions (poses) and so many levels of intensity, yoga is an excellent starting point for developing flexibility and strength. In addition, it has many options for working around chronic problems and physical limitations. Most towns and gyms have yoga studios or classes.

Yoga can also provide a way to spend quality time with your horse—or, more accurately, *on* your horse—as there are specialized programs for "yoga on horseback." These workouts incorporate stretching and bending while mounted, either with the horse standing still or while he is walking (and possibly wondering what his human is up to). These are great for general conditioning but even better for developing confidence in the saddle and finding a better balance and position with your partner. In addition, since much of a yoga practice concentrates on becoming calm and regulating your breathing and emotions, it brings you closer to the mental and physical state you want when you are riding.

### Chiropractic

Chiropractic concentrates on the proper alignment of your spine and joints to allow them to function correctly. Chiropractors have an undergraduate degree plus four years of chiropractic college and are licensed medical professionals.

While it is most well-known for treating back pain, chiropractic is also a treatment for headaches, fibromyalgia, and a host of other medical conditions. The chiropractic approach is that the central nervous system runs through the spinal column, with individual nerves running smoothly from the column to a specific organ. A misaligned spine creates a cramped or blocked nerve. That disrupts the communication between the brain, the nerve, and the organ. In that case, the ability of the organ to function properly is compromised. Chiropractic adjustment realigns the spine to permit the communication to flow effectively.

During your first visit, the doctor takes a complete set of X-rays and discusses your current pains and limitations. She'll then set a schedule for adjustments based on your condition. Adjustments are performed with either with hands-on manipulation of your body or through the use of a small, hand-held device called an "activator" that applies a quick, gentle "pop" of pressure on a joint. Your chiropractor might also prescribe exercises to do at home.

## Somatics

Unlike most exercise programs, somatics is not about strengthening muscles. Instead, this is the general term for bodywork that focuses on awareness of your body and its movement. It includes therapies like the Alexander Technique, the Feldenkrais Method, and Rolfing. Somatics helps develop flexibility, balance, relaxation, and control of your body. It is popular with dancers, gymnasts, and others who need to finely tune those abilities. For our age group, its ability to improve our balance is particularly beneficial since balance is one critical ability that erodes as we age.

Somatics involves the "mind-body interface." This is something of a buzzword term in the health and wellness fields. It stems from the understanding that people often "hold" tension and emotions in parts of their body, affecting their movement. Somatic therapies help identify habits of posture and movement stemming from that as well as from purely physical issues and how to correct those habits that are not beneficial. This is done through a series of gentle exercises that change your muscle memory. Many people see improvements in conditions like back pain, sciatica, and disc issues during treatment, as well as reporting improved sleep and less stress.

Generally, during your first visit, the therapist takes photos of you from the front, back, and sides. When you review them, it is often startling to see how "off" your "normal" posture is. You may notice that one shoulder is higher than the other or that you lean forward when you stand. Yet, it feels perfectly normal. While restoring that balance is important for every aspect of your life, as a rider, these imbalances significantly affect your ride.

CHAPTER 7

# Weight and Riding: A Touchy Subject

The statistics are out there: we're fat. About 42 percent of adults are considered obese. Debating the causes is moot; the consequences are not. Our rate of weight-related illnesses is high and is increasing. Diabetes, heart disease, cancer, osteoarthritis, gout, sleep apnea, stroke—the list goes on and on.

Almost all of us decide at some point to go on a diet. We don't like how we look or feel; we know we are not at our best weight, and we decide that dropping a few pounds is a good idea. However, most of us do not consider what our weight should be. We pick a number out of the air, perhaps decide that we want to weigh what we did 15 years ago, or think that dropping 10, 20, or more pounds is what we "need" to do without any facts to back up that number. Before downloading a calorie counter, you need to determine your proper weight range.

While there is no set formula to determine your ideal target weight, there are some guides. The most common is the Body Mass Index (BMI). The BMI uses a height-weight chart to determine the percentage of fat you carry in relation to your height. That translates into a weight range. For the general population, a healthy BMI is 18 percent to 25 percent. Higher scores are considered overweight or obese. People with lower scores often have higher vitamin deficiency rates, osteoporosis, compromised immune systems, anemia, and respiratory and digestive problems. Since it does not factor in your physical activity, body frame, genetics, gender, or age, BMI is regarded as an estimate, although a useful one. Another method that is considered more accurate is the waist-to-height chart. This uses your waist measurement compared to your height to get a body fat estimate. Again, it ignores the many other factors.

Ongoing research into the health of older adults shows that the standard BMI chart may not be accurate for us. A 12-year study of nearly 200,000 people age 65 and older showed that the lowest risk of death was for people with a BMI of 27 percent to 28 percent and that the mortality rate did not rise significantly when the percentage rose as high as 33 percent. Above that percentage, the mortality began to climb. On the lower side of the scale, BMIs as low as 24 percent were good, but the risk of death increased when they were lower than that. The percentage of muscle to body fat seems to be the critical factor in this statistic. Weight and muscle mass are closely aligned at our age. Loss of muscle mass as we age is normal. It's called *sarcopenia*. It starts when we are in our thirties and continues at a rate of 3 to 5 percent every decade. If your BMI is high, your doctor might advise you to lose a few pounds. But weight loss in older people often results in decreased muscle mass. Research shows a higher risk of death in people with significant sarcopenia, regardless of their weight.

While obesity is a concern, nutritionists and doctors say that being underweight is a more serious problem for older women than carrying a few extra pounds. Being underweight at age 65 was linked to poor health and shorter life spans. The life span and general health of overweight (not morbidly obese) and normal-weight women 65 and older are generally the same. Still, many women obsess over their weight. It's led to the development of a food and diet industry that touts quick fixes and a new body in 12 weeks. Those promises are bogus. While calorie-counting is still the baseline for weight loss, research shows it is much more complicated than that.

Constant focus on the scale is generally unhealthy, particularly if you are caught up in the yo-yo cycle. You lose weight as quickly as possible on a short-term diet, then go back to your old eating habits, regain the weight you lost, and start another diet. This endless cycle disrupts your system, leading to fatty liver, high blood pressure, diabetes, and heart disease. The emphasis is now on regular activity and sensible eating with portion control. The rule of thumb is that a healthy, sustainable weight loss is no more than 1 to 2 pounds a week. That's based on a daily nutritionally balanced calorie count of 1,200 to 1,500 calories a day.

If weight is an issue for you, meet with a nutritionist or dietician. Most physicians have little or no training in nutrition. Medical schools offer only one or two courses in the field, and those are almost always electives. Personal trainers generally lack the same level of knowledge and education that nutrition professionals have. Commercial diet programs can help lose weight but are usually only moderately successful in seeing clients maintain the loss for a year or longer.

## RIDING WHEN OVERWEIGHT

The issue of overweight riders has very practical concerns. Statistics show that overweight participants in contact sports have both more injuries and more serious injuries than fit athletes. Translate that into the most common "contact" of riding—falling. A 15-hand horse stands 5 feet high at the withers. Add your height to that, and your head is 7 or 8 feet above the ground when you are in the saddle. Dropping from that height at a standstill is going to hurt. If the horse is moving, the pain and increased risk of injury go up considerably. When you reach our certain age, you don't bounce the way you did when you were younger. Bones and bruises heal more slowly now, too. Factor in the issue of added weight, and you are looking at a greater chance of injury and even slower recovery time.

Being overweight also affects your ability to ride effectively and safely. The proper riding position is that ears, shoulders, hips, elbows, and ankles are close to a straight line. Binge-watch movies with Steve McQueen, Tom Berenger, or Tom Selleck to see beautiful riding posture (as well as nice eye candy). If you are not riding in that balanced position, your horse can never be balanced either.

Overweight riders often have a more difficult time maintaining proper balance and position. They generally have weak core, thigh, hamstring, and glute muscles that don't allow them to hold the proper leg, seat, and posture positions. As a result, they often sit "in an easy chair," leaning backward with their feet in front of them. They are also probably hanging onto the horse's mouth with the reins in order to stay there. A rider in this position is less able to keep her seat if her horse takes an awkward step or shies. The rider is also putting pressure on the wrong spot on the horse's back. When the horse is uncomfortable, he may react with head-tossing, jigging, bucking, and pawing.

Poor riding posture is also a common culprit for causing painful knees. Your upper thighs, calves, and core should balance you. If your knees hurt, they may be holding you in place instead of the other muscles. Your knees are hinges and should not be carrying weight. Carrying weight and pressure is why they ache. Before adjusting your stirrups or trying out a new saddle, check your riding position. A few longeing lessons without stirrups may help pinpoint balance issues.

Excess weight affects your knees out of the saddle, too. Every pound of body weight equals 4 pounds of pressure on your knees. If you are just 10 pounds above your proper weight range, that adds an extra 40 pounds of pressure on your knees, 80 pounds at 20 pounds above proper weight, and 120 pounds of pressure at 30 extra pounds of weight. Excess strain on the knees is a major reason for deterioration, which leads to a need for knee replacements.

There is a lot of discussion about how much weight a horse can carry safely. The 1920 US Cavalry Manual of Horse Management states that horses should carry no more than 20 to 25 percent of their weight. That includes rider, tack, and contents of saddlebags. This means that a 1,000-pound horse can carry between 200 and 250 pounds of rider, tack, and incidentals. The "20 percent rule" has been accepted as gospel for decades, but is it accurate? Pack horses often carry heavy loads. Quarter Horses on ranches have saddles that weigh 40 pounds or more. And John Wayne was no lightweight. But those horses are built for that work and are physically developed to handle the load. Most Thoroughbreds would fail doing those jobs, while Clydesdales would barely notice those weights.

Recent scientific studies support the 20 percent rule. Carrying too much weight affects a horse's ligaments and back and can cause muscle soreness and imbalance. A detailed study in England found that horses with heavy riders showed signs of slight, temporary lameness after just 30 minutes of walking and trotting in a dressage-style pattern. In one case, the ride was cut short because the horse showed lameness during the ride. The study did not speculate on the effects of longer or more frequent rides. Another study showed that the quality of a horse's gait changes as more weight is added with as little as 20 pounds and even more with an additional 40 pounds. In a third study, riders were fitted with weights that added between 15 and 25 percent of their body weight. This study measured respiration and heart rate, not stress on muscles or tendons. The study found the same indications of stress, like tail swishing and head tossing, from horse to horse, but it was not consistent. The same weight with a different rider did not deliver the same action by the horse, leaving the researchers to wonder how much of the stress was created by the rider's movements.

The horse's conformation is another factor in determining how much weight a horse can carry. Jochen Schleese, the master saddle maker of Schleese Saddlery, suggests determining if the horse has enough saddle-support area and weight-bearing surface to accommodate a larger saddle for a larger rider. You need a professional saddle fitter to make that determination. If that is the case, an overweight rider and her horse may still enjoy a comfortable, safe partnership.

# CHAPTER 8

# Fear: **F**orget **E**verything **A**nd **R**un

There's an odd feature of the riding world: women love horses, but the desire to be with horses is often mixed with fear. You love the idea of riding: you dream of ambling through the woods on a trail ride, trotting down centerline in a dressage arena, or flying around the cloverleaf barrel-racing pattern. You take lessons and might even own a horse. But from the time you drive up to the barn until the time you leave, you are afraid. Your heart races, you sweat, you might be in tears. You might not even get out of your car, just turn around and drive home, feeling defeated and humiliated.

It makes no sense, you tell yourself. It's irrational. You ride with a good instructor and good friends. You used to look forward to going to the barn. When you rode as a youngster, nothing bothered you. You jumped, galloped, went bareback. What went wrong? What spooked you?

Maybe you had a bad fall or witnessed someone else's wreck, and you now tremble at the thought of putting yourself in that situation again. You live alone and are financially responsible for yourself and worry about the consequences of being seriously injured or disabled. You might have a medical condition that makes riding riskier. You feel a touch of mortality and realize the accumulation of all the near misses in the past means that sooner or later, your luck will run out. If you are new to horses, you question your ability to learn enough to be competent. You worry about looking foolish. Or maybe there isn't any identifiable reason for your fear. You just don't feel safe.

But even if you feel nauseated and shaky, even if you are bruised or sporting a cast, even if you need surgery or medical treatment for a horse-related mishap, you are determined to get back to the stable and back in the saddle.

If anyone ever needed proof that horses are addictive, this is it. Despite fear and pain, we can't stay away.

Actually, our heightened sense of uncertainty and fear is a normal part of aging. Our brains react to dangerous, challenging, or fear-inducing situations differently as we age. Young people are slower to react to danger and dismiss potential dangers quickly, leading to that sense of immortality they often display. As we age, we react to danger more quickly and release the tension more slowly. Exactly why this happens is uncertain, but it is a measurable activity in the brain.

We are also dealing with a lifetime of stressors. Significant life changes, professional disappointments, personal losses, health problems, financial uncertainty, even changes in our surroundings—like building projects that alter familiar landscapes—shake our sense of security. Some medications produce adverse side effects, like depression or anxiety.

Our worries fall into three categories: *anxieties, fear,* and *phobias.* Although they share characteristics, they are different things.

Anxiety and fear are kissing cousins. Anxiety is our body's natural response to stress. You feel this at some level when you sit down to pay bills, go to a job interview, or stand on the scale after a vacation. Your breathing and heart rate increase, your stomach gets upset, and your body prepares to run away from danger. You are concerned, but you can still function.

Fear is the more extreme of the pair. Fear is the visceral, gut feeling that you need to get away from a situation *Right Now!* It's like your mare bolting at the sight of a blowing plastic bag. Maybe it can't hurt her, but she is not taking that chance. She'll take off and get out of there before it kills her. For people, fear can develop from the progression of lesser concerns that snowball until you stop thinking or acting rationally. A panic attack is the most extreme manifestation of fear. It is a sudden, unpredictable feeling of terror. Your heart pounds, you are nauseated, you can't breathe, and you feel as though you are losing your mind.

Phobias are a specific, abnormal, and irrational apprehension of a particular thing or situation that compels you to avoid it, despite assurances that it is "Not Dangerous." Many people have some form of claustrophobia, a fear of confined spaces. Perhaps you've heard about people totaling their cars because a spider appears on their dashboard (arachnophobia) or who refuse to visit Australia because there are deadly snakes in the Outback (ophidiophobia). Equinophobia is the extreme terror of horses. (While you may have some nerves about horses and equine activities, I'm guessing they are not that extreme!)

When dealing with horses, anxiety is not irrational. If anything, it is a healthy response to the situation. You are, after all, interacting with a creature that weighs half a ton and often has his own ideas about what he wants to do. You are aware of your aging body and the risks from breaks and strains and sprains that are more likely to happen to us than to younger, more flexible riders.

Even experienced riders always have more to learn. For those of us who are beginners or who are returning after a long hiatus, we are even more aware of how little we know or remember. We want to understand everything and do it correctly. We think (or hope) that this knowledge will keep us safer. If you've had a fall or been kicked, bucked off, tossed by a sideways shy, or run over by a horse, you want to know how to avoid a repeat performance. We all have our comfort zones, and there is nothing "good" or "bad" or "silly" about your anxieties. Knowing your comfort zone and the limits of what you can handle before normal anxiety turns into overwhelming fear is the first step toward addressing the problem.

There are also non-physical triggers that create stress and anxiety. When you take up riding, you are stepping into a new situation and a new challenge. No matter how much you want to be involved with horses, you are operating outside your comfort level. Even if you thrive on new experiences, adjusting to a new activity is disconcerting. If you are used to being in control, this is a situation where you are most definitely not entirely in charge, and that is stressful.

Maybe until now, your life has been predictable: caring for your family, going to work, taking the annual vacation at the beach, watching HGTV, attending church services, and window shopping downtown. You have a circle of family, friends, and acquaintances with similar interests and experiences. You enjoy the familiar, comfortable parameters of your life.

Now you are in an alien world of horses and barns, feed stores and hay bales, tack and strange terminology. Chances are that most people at the barn are new acquaintances, so you are also working on new relationships. None of us is as secure or as confident as we pretend to be, and this is a situation where it is hard to bluff it out. The fear of failure or looking like a fool can discourage you from riding or even being at the stable.

You may also be discovering a new self, and for some people, that means discovering a level of accomplishment and self-reliance that you've never experienced before. If you've always lived the passive role of June Cleaver and now you are as independent as Annie Oakley, you may find that this new empowerment is as intimidating as it is exciting.

You might also be getting negative feedback from significant others in your life who don't share your equine passion. They might feel left out of your life or jealous of your excitement about something they find uninteresting. If they are used to hoarding your attention, they might resent it and act accordingly, even unconsciously, to keep things within their comfort zone. From your point of view, you don't want to damage those relationships. You might start to wonder if life would be easier if you dismounted and stepped away from riding.

If you add it all together: the unknowns of a new activity, the chance of injury, leaving your comfort zone, the challenge of self-discovery, negative pressure on relationships—it's not surprising that you get a dry mouth and jumpy nerves.

Studies show that horses pick up on their rider's emotions. Your horse is listening to your cues and responding to your actions and emotions. If you are uncertain or fearful, your horse might decide that it is safer for him to be in charge. This can lead to behavior you don't want. Which, of course, adds to your anxiety and fear. Studies show that fear also affects athletic performance and coordination. That is not surprising. If you are frightened, you struggle to think, much less move. The studies go further to show that fear affects all aspects of our lives beyond the barn and is related to memory problems, confusion, negative thinking, anger, and irritability.

Your subconscious mind plays a significant role in learning how to handle your anxieties. It works to fulfill what you think about. The concept is that "what you focus on expands." Anxious riders think about everything that can go wrong. If you worry that your horse might shy every time you ride past the open barn door in the enclosed arena, you'll tense up even if you don't realize you are doing it. Your horse might start to wonder what's the big deal about the barn door, figure you must know something that he doesn't, and maybe shy. However, if you visualize riding a straight line along the wall and making a nicely flexed turn at the corner, you won't be worrying about what could go wrong. Neither will your horse.

This visualization is the foundation of the "Law of Attraction" and similar motivational practices. When you visualize something, you subconsciously start taking actions to fulfill that expectation. Sports psychologists urge their clients to use this technique at all levels of training and competition. Riders sit on the bumper of their trailer at a show, close their eyes, and mentally ride their event—not only remembering the reining pattern, jump course, or dressage test but also mentally imagining themselves sitting on their horse and feeling every move: hands in position, calves tightening, shoulders back. When the actual competition begins, they are working, in part, with muscle memory. They already know what will happen and what to expect because they've already "been there, done that."

That's easy to say and read, but your comfort level vanishes when you are physically in the saddle. Beginners are acutely aware of their lack of riding skills. You kick your horse in the butt when you swing your leg over, fumble with the stirrups, and grip the reins so tightly that your fingers ache. You are more rigid than a fencepost and as jumpy as a colt that just touched the electric fence. You are very aware of how tenuously you are managing to stay on the horse's back and just how far above the ground you are.

## CONFIDENCE BUILDERS

One of the most positive ways of dealing with anxiety and fear is trusting your ability to handle yourself and your horse. It is important to find an instructor who understands your nervousness and is willing to help you develop your confidence. Being blunt about your fears is an important part of the conversation you have when you are deciding on an instructor. She should understand your concerns and help you develop your confidence. There is no timetable for this. Trying to program results within a pre-set timeframe almost guarantees failure. If you don't accomplish what you planned, you feel pressured to make up lost time, which leads to more pressure and probably more failures. It's a frustrating loop of disappointment that can take all the fun out of riding.

Equally important is getting in good physical shape, as we've discussed in the past few chapters. For riders, that means having a strong core, which are the deep abdominal muscles that act like a rod around which your body is centered. It keeps you properly positioned and balanced, which you need during any ride, but especially when things don't go as planned. If you are centered and strong, you know it and feel it. The likelihood of a fall when the horse does something unexpected is greatly reduced. If your horse trips, shies, or bucks, you are centered in the saddle and can stay there instead of yanking on his mouth, falling onto his neck, or flopping onto the ground. Learn and practice the *one-rein stop* and *emergency dismount*. These can help you stay in or regain control or get off safely if things turn sour. (Links to videos that demonstrate these are at www.ridersofacertainage.com.)

Protective gear is another confidence builder. Always wear a helmet. A protective vest like those worn by eventers and endurance riders protects your chest and back when you fall. Another useful gadget is a "grab strap" (aka "bucking strap" or "Oh s---t strap"). This leather strap fastens onto the D rings of an English saddle. You grab it for extra stability. You may never use it in an emergency, but it's comforting just knowing that it is there. Western saddles, of course, have the saddle horn.

There are dozens of books, articles, online programs, social media groups, and counselors who help anxious riders recognize their worries and deal with them. It may take time to get over your worries. But almost always, your love of horses will win out over your fears.

# PART THREE

# SAFETY AND THE RIDER OF A CERTAIN AGE

# CHAPTER 9

# Protection and Preventing Injury: Balance, Falls, Vests, and Helmets

C limbing onto the back of a 1,000-pound creature with its own ideas and motivations is risky. The only truly bombproof horse is a Breyer model. Even the most careful person can have a mishap in even the most safety-conscious stable. Unplanned dismounts (aka falling) are embarrassing at best, painful and incapacitating at worse. For us, we have additional conditions and considerations that up the ante in dealing with horse-related activities. As Roy Rogers said, "When you're young and fall off a horse, you may break something. When you're my age and you fall off, you splatter."

Falls are one of the leading causes of injuries for seniors. About 25 percent of seniors over the age of 65 fall every year. At age 80, one-half of us fall annually. It is the leading cause of death from injury in people over 65. The National Council on Aging reports that falls by seniors result in 9,500 deaths annually, either from immediate injuries or from complications from broken bones and other trauma.

Many falls result from poor balance. Part of our ability to function day to day, much less ride well, is our level of "proprioception," the term that defines how we sense where we are in space. It is essential for coordination, movement, and balance. Our balance is generated by inner-ear health and other sensory cues. Our brain interprets these cues and sends signals to our muscles to anchor us in space and immediately adapt to changes. Vaulters who perform gymnastics on a cantering horse have acutely sensitive and refined proprioception. On the other hand, those of us who stagger as we pick out our horses' hooves do not.

As we get older, our peripheral vision and other sensory cues decline. We are generally not aware of that loss because it happens gradually. Some studies hint that we are subconsciously aware of that loss and adjust our behavior to compensate. Our patterns of movement become predictable and constant. Our muscle memory locks into a routine of moving in familiar patterns. When we walk, we look down to monitor where our feet are. If the routine changes, we struggle to adjust. We find that standing on tiptoes or on one leg means bracing a hand on a wall or chair. Our brains need more time to process the unfamiliar movement and send the correction to the muscles.

Riders or not, we must consider the dangers of falling and minimize the risks. Developing our balance and core strength makes falling less likely. Physical therapists, senior centers, and online videos teach exercises and techniques to improve balance and proprioception. Our bodies and brains respond well to these exercises.

A research center in Chicago used a treadmill to simulate conditions that cause falls. Participants picked up cues and corrections quickly, as though they were dance moves. The effects lasted for a year after only a single two-hour session. In addition to practicing balance-building exercises, participating in activities like walking on uneven terrain, riding bicycles, dancing, and playing with a hula hoop develop better coordination and balance. Physical therapists recommend teaching yourself to look straight ahead when walking instead of looking down at your feet. That puts your body in a correct, upright position instead of leaning forward, which throws you off balance. It also helps reactivate your peripheral vision.

Some of the exercises we've already discussed can help, too: Pilates and yoga are perhaps the most effective programs for developing the deep core muscles and strength that keep you balanced. Somatic exercises "rewire" your brain patterns and complement the muscle exercises (see pp. 70 and 73). Exercises for your glutes, abs, and hamstrings are also helpful. Even standing on tiptoes or on one leg while you brush your teeth or stand in line at the grocery store improves your strength and balance. As you repeat the exercises, your brain and body coordinate to add the movement to your body's "repertoire."

## SAFETY VESTS

At some point, you can count on having an unplanned dismount. While falling is almost inevitable, you can reduce the likelihood of serious injury. Consider following the lead of event, endurance, and show jumping riders (not to mention rodeo riders) and wear a safety vest. The vests are practical protection for riders of all ages. They absorb the impact from a fall, providing some protection from broken bones, bruised ribs, and—depending on the model—cervical and neck injuries.

There are two styles of vests. Eventers riding the cross-country phase and bull riders are required to wear a hard-shelled vest that fits like a clamshell around their torso. The interior is filled with shock-absorbing material. The vests can withstand the pressure of a jump standard landing on you, a horse rolling over you, or, in the case of rodeo riders, taking a kick from a bronco or a head-butt from an angry bull.

More commonly seen by recreational riders are inflatable vests. These are tethered to the saddle by a strap or lanyard. When you start to fall, the tension against the tether activates the vest, which inflates like an airbag in an automobile. Some styles inflate around the head and neck, providing support for the spine. Inflatable vests should be returned to the manufacturer every year for an inspection.

Like riding helmets, all vests should be replaced every five years because materials degrade over time (and technology advances, which improves the effectiveness of the vest).

Fit is important. The vest should fit over your riding clothes. If you plan on wearing the vest on top of jackets or coats, wear them when fitting the vest. Each manufacturer's sizing is different, and proper fit around the chest is vital. Each brand has its own instructions for measurement. Some people wear both styles, putting the inflatable vest on top of the hard one. Whether that provides more protection depends on the designs of the vests and whether they can both operate optimally when they are layered. Some manufacturers offer a hybrid combo vest with both styles.

## LEARN HOW TO FALL

You can also learn how to fall. (Perhaps how to "land more safely" is a more accurate description.) While you will probably never tumble and roll like a karate student, even knowing the basics of doing that can help protect you. You can do worse than contact a local karate school or gymnastic studio and ask for a few lessons in tumbling. Landsafe is a company started by a former jockey that conducts two-day courses in "how to fall." Primarily designed for eventers and jumpers, they welcome anyone. The courses begin with gentle rolling and progress to more serious drops, but you are not asked to do more than you can safely handle. They also welcome auditors.

## WEAR A SAFETY HELMET

No arguments. No, "I know how to fall." No, "My horse is bombproof." No, "It's my head, and it's my choice."

Wear the bloody helmet.

Brain trauma can occur from a fall as slight as 3 feet. Consider that your head is between 6 and 8 feet above the ground when you come off your horse, and you are probably moving, which increases the severity of the impact.

Riders are 20 percent more likely to have a head injury than a motorcyclist, based on per-hour statistics, and 45 percent of all traumatic brain injuries (TBI) are horse-related. That's more than motorcycles and skiing combined. A single concussion can permanently damage reflexes, attention span, and focus, and may contribute to chronic migraines.

The average TBI costs four million dollars to treat. How good is your health insurance? How long will you need to recover if you ever do? It may be "your" head but consider the larger impact. Consider the loss of income—both yours, and possibly your partner's, if you have one—because someone must take care of you. What happens if you are your only source of income? Will you qualify for Social Security disability? Even if you are eligible, those benefits are not generous, and you will still have high out-of-pocket costs.

Do you have catastrophic health insurance? Insurance companies rarely pay for renovations or modifications to your house to adapt to meet altered physical needs. The same applies for specialized vehicles or vans. Health care plans may not cover the home health nurse and physical therapist or cover only a limited number of visits or treatments. This includes Medicare and supplemental insurance. Without the additional insurance, you are on your own for paying those bills.

What happens to your horse? If you board, who is paying the bills? If you keep your horse at home, who is tending to it? If the horse was injured in the incident, who pays the vet bills? If the horse is "blamed" for the accident, will anyone buy him?

Maybe you must hire an assistant. Kiss your retirement savings goodbye. Sell your house and all the memories inside and find a modified place to live.

How will this trauma affect your family and friends? Will your kids have to disrupt their lives, their careers, and their finances to care for you? Do you want to ride with your grandkids, go on vacation with them, or even be alive to watch them grow?

What about your job? How will your employer and coworkers deal with your absence? What if you are the business owner? Who runs your business? What happens to your employees if your business shuts down?

Do you want an example of how it can go so wrong, so quickly? Consider Courtney King-Dye. An Olympic medalist, top of her field, superb horsewoman. A young horse she was training tripped, they both fell, and her head hit the ground hard. She was not wearing a helmet. She spent weeks in a coma and months in therapy learning how to dress herself again, eat, and perform daily tasks without help. A YouTube video shows how she now struggles to speak and her lack of dexterity and coordination as she tries to open a bottle of aspirin, take the pills, stand, and walk. On her blog, Courtney describes the depression she deals with as she adjusts to her new reality.

Wear the bloody helmet.

As I discussed earlier in the book, your helmet must be ASTM/SEI certified. These are standards set by the American Society for Testing and Materials (ASTM) and the Safety Equipment Institute (SEI). The helmet must offer several forms of protection. It must absorb the impact from the fall so that your brain does not slam into your skull at full speed; it must resist crushing or penetration due to kicking, a loose spike from a shoe, or a tree branch; it must allow only minimal distortion and must return to nearly its original dimensions after pressure is removed. A helmet that does not meet these international safety standards may not offer any more protection than a baseball cap. That old velvet helmet sitting in your attic or you found at a yard sale is not going to work.

New technology is making helmets even safer. MIPS (Multi-directional Impact Protection System) technology mimics your brain's own protection system. Developed by brain surgeons and scientists, it's an insert that fits inside your helmet. It rotates to absorb the pressure and impact that would otherwise directly hit your brain. It does not affect the fit or feel of the helmet. As of the time of writing, manufacturers are starting to offer it in some models.

## MEDICAL ALERT SYSTEMS: HOW TO CALL FOR HELP

In addition to falling, there are dozens of potential injury-inducing situations around the barn that can be as serious as falling from your horse. Many of us are at the barn, on the trail, in the field, or in the arena when no one else is around. Sooner or later, someone will find us, but it could be hours, perhaps critical hours. If you rely on your cell phone for communication, you must be sure it is on you—and reachable—at all times. On trail rides, in particular, people put their cell phone in their saddlebag, making it useless should they fall and their horses trot away.

Over 450,000 people are taken to emergency rooms each year, unconscious and without identification. If nothing else, carry your ID on you with your name and information and emergency contact. If you have a critical medical condition, wear a medical alert bracelet. ROADiD is a company that offers a wristband with your basic contact information on the front and a link and telephone number on the back. That connects to a database with your pertinent medical and contact information.

Many people carry their cell phones with them and think this is a sure way to call for help, be it at the barn or on the trail. Despite the proliferation of cell towers popping up like mushrooms after the rain, there are still many areas with poor cell reception. Relying on a cell phone for emergency communication is not the best idea. However, even if you do not have a signal on your phone, dial 911. Your carrier might not have coverage in that area, but other carriers might, and your 911 call will be routed through them. The cell towers can triangulate your position.

You should also include ICE on your cell phone. ICE stands for "In Case of Emergency." This is a list of emergency contacts available to first responders and medical personnel if you cannot communicate. Even if your phone is locked, most systems allow access to ICE contacts. Check with your phone carrier and manufacturer about setup.

A medical alert system will call for help in most situations if you are injured or have an emergency. There are several options. Some are specifically designed for falls, while others activate for many other emergencies. Some simply direct responders to your location, while others allow for conversations with the rescuers. Almost all alert systems require a monthly fee.

The basic medical alert system is probably the most well-known. In an emergency, you press a button on a pendant worn around your neck or a device on your wrist. That sends a signal to a dispatch center. Almost all these systems offer two-way communications so that the dispatcher can stay with you until help arrives. In general, these systems operate around the house. The transmitter has a very short range generally too limited to be useful at the barn or on a trail.

If you have reliable cell or WiFi service, a smartwatch with medical alert apps is the most practical solution. They operate anywhere with a signal, so if you are in the barn and throw out your back while loading hay or get lost on a trail far from home, you can summon help.

Other alert systems are specifically designed to respond to falls. Some devices monitor the proximity of horse and rider and activate if you two become separated. They send an SOS to a contact that you have programmed into the device settings. They also track the horse if he wanders away from you. Other systems monitor your movement. If they detect no activity for several minutes, the device sets off a warning, and if you don't turn it off, it contacts emergency services. (One system includes an option for attaching a theft protection device to your trailer. If your trailer moves when you haven't deactivated the alert, it contacts authorities.)

Emergency locators are popular with those who ride off the beaten track or where there is no cell service. A Personal Locator Beacon (PLB) sends a message to rescue agencies and pinpoints your location when you hit the SOS button. You must register with NOAA (National Oceanic and Atmospheric Administration) with your personal contact information, emergency contacts, and medical conditions. A satellite messenger sends an SOS and allows for two-way communication and the ability to cancel the SOS.

# CHAPTER 10

# When to Quit:
# Questions to Ask and Options

At age 101, Connie Reeves went for her daily ride. As they started to canter, her "lively" horse, Dr. Pepper, threw her. She was medevacked to a hospital but died of her injuries a few days later. The possibly apocryphal version of the story claims that as the medics loaded her into the chopper, she commented, "Somehow, I had hoped that my last dismount would not have been so dramatic."

At age 68, Mary Burger won her second title as the World Champion Barrel Racer in the Women's Professional Rodeo Association. Julie Suhr is a legend in the endurance riding world, competing in her 90s. Fox hunts routinely count members in their sixties and above, as does eventing. In Australia, Joan Sinclair works cattle on her ranch in the High Country as she nears 90. The US Dressage Federation awards membership into the Century Club for a horse-and-rider team whose combined age is over 100. At 95, Ginny Wegener rode her 27-year-old Fjord, Solveig, for her third USDF Century Ride.

And let us not forget HM Queen Elizabeth II, who well into her nineties, regularly hacks her dependable black Fell Pony, Carltonlima Emma, around the Great Park grounds at Windsor Castle.

We start riding lessons in our sixties and buy a new horse for our seventieth birthday. We brag about still cinching saddles and hacking out in our eighties. We sit in our saddle and pray, "Dear Lord, never let me know the last time I ride a horse."

As much as we want that to be true, riding until we draw our last breath might not be possible. Physical issues may make it impossible to climb into the saddle. It could be a judgment call. Is riding going to turn a marginal health issue into a serious one? Does your stubborn determination to keep riding outweigh your common sense?

If you are asking those questions, you may have already answered them. Have a heart to heart with your instructor and your friends. Ask them to be blunt. They may have noticed things you've missed or ignored. Talk with your family and doctor. You may have to change your routine, change the type of riding you do, or ride less frequently.

If you decide that being in the saddle is no longer safe, practical, or possible, there's no reason to leave the horse world. The variety and challenges of groundwork are different kinds of fun. The non-ridden equine movement, which I touched upon at the beginning of the book, provides many options for enjoying horses without riding. Set up cavalletti or an obstacle course; try the sport of Horse Agility. Learn to "speak" horse, using books and videos about understanding horse body language and herd dynamics. Discover equine bodywork. Develop a freestyle choreography at liberty. A walk along a trail with your horse on a lead line develops a bond at a different level. Some people take up driving—learning how to hitch a horse to a wagon, cart, or trap. Volunteer at a rescue, where a knowledgeable helper is always welcome. Get involved with equine-assisted therapy, perhaps become a therapist yourself. Even just sitting in a beach chair reading a book while your horse grazes nearby is a lovely way to pass an afternoon.

Being out of the saddle does not mean leaving the horse world!

# PART FOUR

# UNIQUELY OURS: HEALTH ISSUES THE KIDS DON'T FACE

# CHAPTER 11

# What Changes with the Years

Here we are, living our happy lives, reaching the apex of our career or enjoying retirement, spoiling our grandkids, indulging in our new-found love of horses, and *wham,* we start having medical problems. All of us expect the occasional setback, but sometimes it seems as though there is a cosmic plan to sabotage our riding with a run of ailments and complications.

Our bodies change as we age. We're no longer night owls; nine o'clock is the new midnight. We creak when we get up in the morning (and during the night for trips to the loo). Our stamina, balance, and coordination are not as robust or dependable as they once were. Workouts with jumping jacks and squat sets make our knees ache.

Those are the changes we recognize. What we don't see is how our bones are losing density and becoming weaker and how deteriorating sensory traits like hearing and vision affect our physical abilities. But knowledge is power, and knowing the basics of common conditions we face helps us understand our options in dealing with them.

While they are annoying, few health problems are so debilitating that they force you permanently out of the saddle. Most can be managed, if not completely fixed, but that doesn't dismiss the frustration and anger that comes from feeling as though your body has betrayed you. It's small comfort to know that many other women our age also struggle. Still, there is something to be said for getting together with other ladies to share stories of medical misery while indulging in wine and chocolate and planning a group horse camping trip.

## MENOPAUSE

This is the one condition that all women share regardless of race, religion, ethnic background, political affiliation, marital status, geographic location, career field, economic status, or education. At the same time, it is a very individual condition, with each woman having her own unique experience. As horse people, the changes and symptoms can interfere with our physical comfort, our emotional balance, our ability to focus, and the simple pleasure of being with our horses.

Technically, "menopause" is the term used to describe your condition 12 months *after* your last period. Until then, it's officially "perimenopause" ("peri" meaning "before") or "the menopausal transition." Most people, however, routinely refer to the entire process as "going through menopause," "change of life," or, most quaintly, "going through 'The Change.'" It usually lasts about seven years and starts, on average, at age 51.

Menopause is Mother Nature's way of shutting down our reproductive system. As we get older, our bodies produce less estrogen and progesterone. These are the hormones that regulate our fertility. This process starts in our thirties and continues until our ovaries stop producing eggs. There is no known reason why the process can't simply happen in a couple of weeks and be over and done with. Mother Nature has a strange sense of humor.

The list of symptoms is long, well-discussed, and usually uncomfortable. It includes, in no particular order: irregular periods, hot flashes, night sweats, mood swings, weight gain, thinning hair, loss of libido, chills, depression, tender breasts, and vaginal dryness.

On the plus side, once you are through menopause, you no longer deal with periods, cramps, or worrying about an unexpected pregnancy. On the downside, you now have an increased chance of heart disease, osteoporosis, urinary incontinence, sexual discomfort, and weight gain.

There are actually a few books about the joys of menopause written by doctors and counselors who smile beatifically from the covers of their books. It is a wonderful time, they proclaim, when you rediscover yourself and can celebrate the second half of your life. They recommend embracing the physical elements as a sign of the new you who is about to arrive. It is not known if any of those authors made these statements to a woman on a day when she was dealing with rampant bleeding, bloating, and the desire to dismember the driver who just cut her off in traffic.

Irregular periods are often the first sign of starting menopause. You may skip a month or two, have a period every two weeks, spot off and on, or bleed continually or for longer than usual. When this starts, a visit to your gynecologist is in order. She may run tests to confirm that you are beginning the transition and rule out other causes. Those screenings can include a D&C, thyroid tests, blood tests, and a colonoscopy. All of those are prudent procedures for all women our age, even if we are not enduring other symptoms.

There is no "treatment" for menopause except time. However, there are ways to deal with the symptoms. The most common is Hormone Replacement Therapy (HRT). It's also called Menopausal Hormone Therapy (MHT) or Estrogen Replacement Therapy (ERT). These are pills, patches, creams, ointments, and sprays that increase your estrogen and progesterone levels. Your gynecologist should listen to your symptoms and discuss the options, including the pros, cons, side effects, and benefits of each treatment, so you are well-informed. Feel confident to ask many questions and get explanations until you are comfortable with your knowledge and can decide on the treatment that sounds like the best approach to your situation.

A word here about Premarin. This was, and still is, a common source of estrogen. The word comes from three others: Pregnant Mare's Urine. Mares are bred specifically to produce the hormone. The hormone-laden urine is collected in bags that are attached to the mares during their pregnancies. During that time, the mares are confined to stalls. The foals, which are the by-product of the process, are considered expendable. These are called "PMU foals." The lucky ones are adopted or sent to rescue. Unfortunately, many of them are not and are slaughtered. Their dam is immediately bred again, and the cycle repeats.

For many years, there were few options for Premarin, but there are now synthetic substitutes. For some women, the equine-derived version is the only effective relief, but ask your doctor for other treatment options. Don't be surprised if your doctor does not know where Premarin comes from. Many do not.

There are "natural" and "alternative" therapies for menopausal symptoms. These include botanicals (diet and herbal supplements derived from plants), acupuncture, chiropractic, massage therapy, and biofeedback techniques. Some studies indicate that black cohosh, soy, flaxseed, cold drinks, and vitamin E ease hot flashes and night sweats. Laying off caffeine is almost universally recommended. Yoga, exercise, structured breathing, and swimming also bring relief from mood swings and sleep disruption for some women. You can try different techniques and see what works. Since none of these is invasive, they are generally not harmful. Ultimately, though, it takes time. A lot of time.

## POST-MENOPAUSAL PROBLEMS

### Osteoporosis and Osteopenia

One of the concerns of riders at any age is breaking something—wrists, legs, hips, collar bones. More than most other sports, riders have the unfortunate and un-planned tendency to learn more about their skeletal systems than they would like. For younger people, it's often an abstract possibility, and they usually heal fairly quickly after an accident. For us, however, age-related physical changes increase the likelihood of fractures.

*Osteoporosis*, which means "porous bone," is a condition in which the density of your bones is reduced. *Osteopenia* is a less serious version of the same condition. Both are factors in the chances of suffering bone fractures. Although osteoporosis is more severe, more fractures are seen in people with osteopenia because more people have this condition.

I've mentioned already that as we age, we lose bone density. We lose between 3 and 12 percent per decade, depending on which bones are being measured. By the time we are 80, we've lost one-third of our hip bone density. About 50 percent of us will break a bone because of osteopenia or osteoporosis. The biggest risks are for broken wrists, spines, and hips. Broken hips are most common.

Loss of estrogen and the leaching of calcium and other minerals from our bones after menopause make our bones more brittle. Low levels of Vitamin D are also a significant factor. The body absorbs Vitamin D from sunlight. Unfortunately, unless you live on the equator, you don't get enough exposure to sunlight to absorb the right amounts. To ensure you are getting enough Vitamin D, you need to take supplements. Vitamin D also helps brain function and appears to help stave off "senior moments" and improve balance.

To find out how well your skeleton is dealing with aging, get a bone density test. Everyone over age 65 should have one. Post-menopausal women over the age of 50 and anyone who has broken a bone after age 50 should have one, too. The test, called a DEXA scan, is quick and painless. It measures the bone density in your hip, spine, and wrists because those are the most common locations for fractures. The results allow your physician to predict your future risk for fractures.

Strength and weight training are proven ways to increase bone density. Some studies indicate that weight-bearing exercises not only maintain existing bone strength but also helps bones to rebuild some lost density. The training also strengthens muscles and improves coordination, which improves balance and lessens the chances of falling and breaking bones.

### Weight Gain

After menopause, your metabolism slows. This means that you need fewer calories to function, and it is harder to burn off the extras. Once again, the loss of estrogen is the trigger for the situation. There are other factors, too, like loss of muscle mass, inadequate sleep, and insulin resistance.

Many women find that they have smaller appetites after menopause. That big meal you once looked forward to now leaves you feeling bloated instead of satisfied. Some women find life is more enjoyable if they eat smaller and more frequent meals. Like their horses, they gently nibble and graze all day. Nutritionists say that eating something every three to four hours is ideal for maintaining our blood sugar levels and keeping our appetites in check. Snacks are not chips, dips, or Thin Mints, but a handful of nuts, a piece of fruit, or yogurt. (Read the labels. Most commercial yogurts are full of sugar and are not much different than melted ice cream.) Reducing sweets, alcohol, and junk food removes many empty calories that were hard to work off even before menopause.

Very few studies about weight reduction programs look specifically at peri- or postmenopausal women. Those studies which show successful results are versions of the modified/lower carb diets. There are no statistics specifically for women of menopausal age, but overall, people in the 55 and over age bracket lost body fat when following those programs. When followed correctly, dieters lost pounds, body fat, and inches on their waistlines. At the same time, their metabolic numbers improved. They also found it easier to maintain their new eating habits and weight loss when they reached their initial goals.

We touched on the issue of weight and riding in chapter 7 (p. 74). While post-menopausal weight gain is not likely to be so significant as to affect your horse's ability to carry you, it can impact your balance and comfort in the saddle. Things that were once easy can seem awkward until you become familiar with your changed body. Transitions of any kind are rarely easy, but there is plenty of horse fun still to be had on the other side.

# CHAPTER 12

# Bouncing, Chafing, Leaking, and Arthritis

## BRAS

Many of us discover that, along with joy and fulfillment, riding often means trying to keep "The Girls" in place and dealing with discomfort in our private parts.

You don't want parts of you to keep bouncing when your horse stops moving. If nothing else, constantly bouncing "mammaries" hurt long after you dismount. From a riding perspective, the jiggling throws off your balance, particularly if you are well-endowed. It's also embarrassing when The Girls escape the confines of your bra while you are riding. Victoria's Secret be damned; this is one time when you want to minimize your cleavage.

Sports bras are the obvious answer. A bra designed for tennis players was introduced in 1975, but the first sports bra was created in 1977 by Lisa Lindal, Polly Smith, and Hinda Schreiber Miller at the University of Vermont. They sewed together two jock straps for a prototype and refined the idea from there. One of the original bras was bronzed and is on display at the university. Two others are displayed at The Smithsonian and the New York Metropolitan Museum of Art, proving how important sports bras are to society!

With wide straps and solid coverage over a wide area, sports bras hold everything relatively immobile while allowing freedom of movement. There are several styles. Besides the customary cut, there are camisoles that are a little longer than the usual bra, and bra-tank combos that come down to your waist. Some bras have a front zipper or a rear hook-and-eye closure like regular bras; others are solid pieces of fabric with no closures and require you to perform upper-body gymnastics to wriggle into them. Another product is a strap that fits across the top of your bust line to keep your breasts from bouncing.

Like everything else with clothing, sizing is more of a suggestion than a direction. A few brands have cup and width sizes. Otherwise, the choices are S, M, L, XL, XXL. Some retailers' websites have sizing charts that roughly match the letter size with cup and width sizing. If you don't live near a store that sells sports bras, you need to order online. Most of the horse-oriented sites that sell clothing also carry bras.

## PANTIES AND UNDERGARMENTS

Many women complain about chafing after riding. They wonder if they should adjust their stirrups, apply liberal amounts of ointments, or buy foam or wool seat cushions.

The first thing to consider is the saddle fit. Saddle fit is just as vital for you as it is for your horse. Like shoes, saddles have different widths and designs. A saddle might fit your horse perfectly but be unsuitable for you. The seat might be too large or too small, the twist too narrow or too wide, or the saddle too long or too short. Any of these flaws can force your body into a position that puts your crotch in a vulnerable position and prevents you from balancing correctly. Poor riding posture also causes aching knees, backaches, and hip pain. Sitting in the wrong position is also uncomfortable for your horse, who can react by jigging, bucking, pulling on the reins, or performing other objections.

Most saddles are unisex in their design, which means both men and women can use them. However, a woman's pelvis is significantly wider than a man's, something that few saddle makers consider. The typical design means it is more difficult for women to maintain proper posture. Only a few brands design saddles specifically for women.

For both English and Western riding, you should be sitting evenly on your seat bones. This allows your ear, shoulder, hips, and ankles to be in a straight line. You should not see your toes when you look down. With the dozens of different saddle models available, women working with an experienced fitter can usually find a saddle that meets their needs, which may solve the chafing problem.

After you evaluate your saddle and riding position, consider what you are wearing. In general, you want a breathable fabric, like microfiber, which wicks away moisture and doesn't bunch up like cotton. Avoid seams along the inner thigh and crotch. Look for seamless underpants. Boxer shorts are popular, and the fan club of Hanes Comfort Briefs for Men swear that they are a blessing and do not bulge in any embarrassing way.

Padded panties are also popular. Some brands are made specifically for riders, but padded biking shorts and compression shorts have their followers. Padded seating is another option, with neoprene, gel pads, memory foam, fleece, and wool for both English and Western saddles.

Half a dozen different anti-chafing creams and gels are available in drugstores and online. Other people slather on diaper-rash cream or that old reliable, Vaseline. Be careful, though; some of these products stain clothing and could ruin those $200 breeches.

## URINARY INCONTINENCE

You ride, and you dribble. You're grooming your horse, and without warning, you leak. You're hooking up your trailer and need to scoot into the back to pee in the shavings.

It's embarrassing, but you are not alone.

Urinary incontinence can happen to any woman at any age, but it is most common for us. There are several reasons. Our bladder and pelvic floor muscles weaken with age as the warranty on our bodies expires. Another common cause is Urinary Tract Infections (UTIs). Arthritis is yet another culprit. If you are less active and more sedentary because of pain and stiffness, the muscles that control your bladder become weaker from lack of use.

The most extreme version of these weaknesses is "pelvic organ prolapse." This happens when the bladder, rectum, or uterus shifts out of position. This prevents the bladder and urethra from operating normally. While there are some non-invasive treatments for this, surgery is sometimes the only way to completely solve the problem.

Different types of urinary incontinence are typical for our age group. *Stress incontinence* is the most common. This happens when pressure is put on the bladder, like cantering or posting, lifting hay bales, or dragging jump standards into position. This is also the version responsible for peeing when you laugh or sneeze.

*Urge incontinence* happens when you must pee *right now* and can't hold it long enough to reach a bathroom. There is no warning about this. Often, it happens when you've recently had a lot of water or caffeine to drink and you may be overhydrated, but it can happen at any time for no apparent reason. For some women, it's a regular occurrence; for others, it's just an occasional, unwelcome surprise.

*Functional incontinence* happens to people who usually have normal bladder control. They have trouble getting to the bathroom "in time" because they move more slowly and cannot get back to the barn or off the horse fast enough.

Even if incontinence is just an occasional situation, visit your doctor. Checking this out might uncover other issues before they become serious. At our age, getting a fast start on medical conditions is always a positive action. Your primary care physician is a good start, but a urologist is better.

In the meantime, using absorbent underwear is a solution. In addition to several disposable brands, there are new brands specifically for dealing with urinary incontinence. Those have the additional benefit of having padding, which helps deal with chafing.

## ARTHRITIS AND SPARE PARTS

Many orthopedic surgeries address spinal, cervical, and other conditions. How these affect your ability to ride is far outside the scope of this book. What I will address are the general conditions concerning knee and hip replacements.

Creaking knees, stiff backs, and tight hips are the normal start of the day for many of us. Bending over to pick out hoofs and straightening up afterward may mean leaning on your horse to get leverage. Swinging your leg over the saddle is a major effort, and your back complains during the first mile of your trail ride. Your knees complain loudly when you dismount. These are often the signs of osteoarthritis, the "wear-and-tear" arthritis. It happens to most of us as we age.

Arthritis is the loss of cartilage at the joint. Cartilage is the hard, slippery tissue that covers the ends of bones at a joint. As this wears out and wears off, bone begins to rub against bone. That's when the pain, swelling, stiffness, redness, and decreased range of motion begin. While any joint can be affected, hips, knees, hands, fingers, and wrists are usually the most common and the most painful.

There are over 100 different types of arthritis, but osteoarthritis is the most common. A family history of the condition, age, weight, and old injuries are all risk factors. Repetitive motion activities and high-impact activities (like riding hunters and jumpers) are also culprits.

For minor cases, taking over-the-counter medications, applying heat or ice, and using weight training to strengthen muscles around the joints are usually effective. The Arthritis Foundation recommends exercise as the most effective non-drug treatment for reducing pain and improving movement. Losing weight takes pressure off joints, especially knees. Acupuncture provides relief for many patients, and chiropractic treatments are helpful for some types of arthritis. Cortisone shots and injections of hyaluronic acid may also provide relief.

At some point, however, the temporary fixes can stop working, and joint replacements are in order. Each year, there are about 500,000 knee replacements and 175,000 hip replacements. That number increases yearly because our generation refuses to act our age by living sedentary lives. Active people like riders are considered good candidates for replacement because we are generally in good overall physical health, are motivated, and have leg strength.

Many well-intentioned surgeons don't understand our obsessive need to ride. They will tell you that your days in the saddle are over. They do not understand that with a few specific exceptions, like jumping, riding is generally a non-load-bearing sport. With conscientious physical therapy, you have an excellent chance of riding after surgery.

Follow advice as to therapy and take the time you need to heal. You'll probably feel fine long before your body has completely recovered. With some of the newest hip replacements, you can be close to full normal activities in a week or so. Keep in mind that "normal" in this context means things like walking around the block, grocery shopping, and dusting the house, not going on a trail ride, even a short one.

You don't have to give up your stable time while you heal. Hand graze or refine your groundwork. When you ride again, pay attention to your body. Let your instructor help pinpoint changes in the way you are sitting and moving. If you are struggling, back off and give yourself more time to heal and return gradually.

# CHAPTER 13

# Vision, Sleep, Hearing, and Breathing

## VISION CHANGES

It starts in your forties. You notice that you must hold books farther away and need more light to read the pages. It's harder to judge distances when you are driving at night. You don't notice things in your peripheral vision. You need more time to adjust to sudden light changes, like leaving the shadows of the barn and stepping into the bright riding ring. You squint to see the holes in your stirrup leathers.

Like everything else that starts to wear out as we age, vision loss is another challenge. The National Eye Institute says that one in three of us lose some vision by the time we're 65. Even before you notice symptoms, schedule an eye exam with an optometrist. You should have one every year starting in your forties, but certainly every year once you hit 60.

The most common condition for aging eyes is *presbyopia*, a decrease in sharpness and other visual abilities. This is the condition that has you buying reading glasses at CVS, losing them, and buying and misplacing another pair and another until there are a half-dozen reading glasses scattered around your house. (And you can't find any of them.) Nothing can reverse the condition, and it will probably grow worse over time. Eventually, you may need to wear prescription glasses or contacts.

*Reduced pupil size* is another age-related vision condition. The muscles that control size and reaction to light lose strength. This is what causes the loss of night vision. From age 69 onward, we need three times more ambient lighting for reading than we did in our twenties. There's nothing that can be done to correct this.

*Loss of peripheral vision* is another common condition. We lose between one to three degrees of peripheral vision each decade. By our seventies, we've lost between 20 and 30 degrees of our side vision. In the barn, loss of peripheral vision might keep you from seeing where you are in relation to a horse. You can end up being stepped on or causing a spook. Loss of peripheral vision is particularly hazardous when driving. All cars have blind spots to begin with, and the loss of peripheral vision means we are more likely to miss seeing vehicles beside and behind us. That's particularly dangerous when you are towing a trailer. Train yourself to turn your head and look behind you and to the side. Don't just trust your mirrors when merging, yielding, turning, or changing lanes.

## SLEEP ISSUES

Older women need between seven to eight hours of sleep per night. Often, however, we try to maintain the same lifestyle as when we were younger and had a reserve of extra energy to draw on. We stay up late to watch a movie when our bodies require that we turn out the lights earlier. Many seniors sleep only four to six hours a night, and often that is broken into shorter periods. This isn't the lack of sleep that comes from sitting up all night waiting for a foal to be born or the sudden wake-up when a neighbor calls to tell you that your horses got out and are trotting down the road. This is the nightly routine of waking several times or sleep-

**AGELESS ADVICE**

## *Habits to Get the Best Sleep*

➤ Develop a consistent routine of when you go to bed each night and get up each morning. Include some time for a mental "cooldown." Play quiet music, read a book, meditate, practice a bedtime yoga routine, write in a journal.

➤ Make your bedroom a quiet, dark, comfortable sanctuary.

➤ Avoid alcohol, caffeine, bedtime snacks, and nicotine after dinner.

➤ Avoid afternoon naps.

➤ Avoid leaving your computer or cell phone turned on in your bedroom. The blue light cast by electronic devices is shown to disrupt sleep patterns.

➤ Deal with snoring. You might not realize that you snore unless your partner tells you. But loud snorers usually don't go through the entire sleep cycle and are often only dozing. When your snoring is so loud that it wakes you or has forced your partner to sleep in another room, consider getting a sleep assessment. Depending on the cause, changing your sleeping positions, using over-the-counter sleeping devices, using a C-PAP machine, or having minor surgery to remove part of your soft palate can help.

ing so lightly that you wake if a gnat sneezes a mile away. Visiting the loo a time or two doesn't help, either.

Too little sleep depresses your immune system, leads to mental confusion and decreased ability to concentrate, contributes to lack of coordination and the risk of falling, and can affect your mood by making you as crabby as a chestnut Thoroughbred mare in season.

## HEARING LOSS

One in three people between the ages of 65 and 75 has some degree of hearing loss. Once you reach age 75, that number climbs to 50 percent. Everyone 50 or older should have their hearing screened to discover problems before they are serious. An audiologist or hearing aid specialist can perform the screening, as can an ear/nose/throat specialist MD.

Hearing loss starts gradually. The normal level of TV audio is too low. You struggle to hear your instructor clearly if she's on the other side of the ring.

There are many options for treating hearing loss, including hearing amplification devices and surgical treatments like implants. New hearing aids for slight to moderate hearing loss, available over the counter without a prescription, are starting to be marketed.

## RESPIRATORY ISSUES

While our lungs do not age, they are affected by age-related changes elsewhere in our bodies. Our bones contract, which means our rib cage shrinks, and our lungs cannot expand as much as they once did. Our diaphragm muscles also weaken. That's why we get winded more easily and need more time to get our breath back after exertion like hauling water buckets or riding a canter. Regular cardiovascular exercise is both a preventive and an effective treatment to keep the lungs strong.

Chronic respiratory diseases are the third most common cause of death for people over age 65. The two most common forms are chronic bronchitis and emphysema. In both cases, symptoms include wheezing, coughing, and shortness of breath. Asthma, which shares similar symptoms, affects more than two million seniors. It's important to get an accurate diagnosis if you have any of those symptoms to receive proper treatment.

# PART FIVE

# BUT HE'S SO PRETTY: BUYING A HORSE (OR NOT)

# CHAPTER 14

# Shopping for a Horse: What Are You Looking for and Where Do You Find It?

While the excitement of physically demanding equestrian sports like endurance and eventing attract some people, most older riders generally take up more sedate disciplines. There are only a few activities where the breed matters. Unless you ride in one of them, your horse's bloodline and pedigree don't matter.

There is no "ideal" breed for an older rider (or any rider for that matter). Many breeds have general characteristics, but they are just that—general. Every horse is an individual. A horse of a breed that's known for its easy-going nature can be a firecracker, while a horse from a "hot" breed can be an in-your-lap "snuggler." You want a horse who's a good partner with a good personality and disposition. You want a horse at your skill level; a horse who will help you develop is ideal, but avoid getting a horse you can "grow into." A novice or returning rider needs a reliable teacher, not a green horse or one with more challenges than you can handle. As the saying goes, "Green on green makes black and blue."

## APPROPRIATE BREEDS TO CONSIDER

For older riders, particularly those of us new to riding or returning after years out of the saddle, most instructors suggest the *American Quarter Horse*. It's the most popular breed in the United States, with over three million horses registered with the American Quarter Horse Association. The name comes from its ability to sprint over short distances, like a quarter mile. They are the horses used on ranches and rodeos. When you watch a Western movie, the cowboys, cavalry, and Native Americans are probably riding Quarter Horses.

It's often said that Quarter Horses are "born broke" because they are intelligent, patient, easy to train, and have great personalities. They are sturdy, generally easy keepers, and not prone to illness. For those who are a bit fearful of being far off the ground, Quarter Horses are mid-height, usually 14.2 to 15.2 hands. They are also versatile and adapt to all disciplines: trail riding, dressage, jumping, eventing, and all the traditional Western jobs and rodeo sports. Their "been there, done that" attitude and calm nature instill confidence in uncertain and inexperienced riders.

You'll hear the terms "Appendix" and "Foundation" Quarter Horses. The AQHA allows Quarter Horses to be bred with Thoroughbreds and they are called "Appendix." Initially, this was to produce faster horses to race on Quarter Horse tracks, although nowadays, many of these horses are used for recreational riding and never see a starting gate. A "Foundation" Quarter Horse has very little, if any, Thoroughbred in its bloodline. Many people consider "Foundation" Quarter Horses to be the most authentic representative of the breed. They are very reliable and almost frighteningly intelligent horses.

Several other breeds share traits with the Quarter Horse. *Paints* have a lot of Quarter Horse in their pedigree. They are intelligent, good-looking, and easy to train. Like the Quarter Horse, they stand between 14 and 15 hands.

*Appaloosas*, with their distinctive spots, are another good all-around breed. The *Connemara Pony* is sometimes called the "Irish Quarter Horse." Smaller than their American cousins, standing about 14 hands, they are gentle and patient, and love human interaction. *Morgans* are popular as a family horse and a good partner for beginners. They are easy keepers, and health issues are rare. They stand at about 14 and 15 hands. *Friesians* are black horses with distinctive feathers on their legs and dramatic, flashy movement. They have the personality of Labrador Retrievers and are eager to please their riders. Even though they stand only 15.3 on average, their big movement can intimidate new riders. Pricey but wonderful, *Lusitano* horses are also known for their great personalities and patience. They are appreciated for their ability to concentrate and adapt to their rider's abilities. The hearty *Haflinger*, which stands only between 13 and 15 hands, is a sturdy, dependable mount.

"*Grade horses*" are crossbreeds—horses with mixed parentage from two or more breeds. They usually reflect the best qualities of the breeds of each of their parents. Often, they are horses with no known pedigree, and guessing the breeds involved is similar to guessing the parentage of a mixed breed dog. They are often less expensive than registered horses. In some cases, crossbreeding is a deliberate effort to breed for specific performance, behavior, or confirmation traits.

You'll get lots of advice about the qualities and traits of different breeds. You'll hear that *Thoroughbreds* and *Arabians* are "hot" and are a handful, yet many OTTB (Off-the-Track Thoroughbreds and retired racehorses) have great careers as jumpers and dressage horses, and many of them are happy on trails. Arabians are legendary for their stamina and are the stars in endurance events.

A *Warmblood* can be a horse of a specific breed or one that meets the requirements of a registry. They originated in Europe as crosses between heavy horses used for farm work and the lighter, livelier "hot" horses. To be accepted into a registry, a horse must meet specific characteristics in appearance and behavior. Horses are bred for performance goals, generally as sport horses in show jumping, dressage, eventing, or driving. Only the *Trakehner* registry requires a pure bloodline. *Holsteiner, Hanoverian*, and *Selle Français* require that one of the breeding stock be of that breed. Among the other Warmblood breeds and registries are *Dutch Warmblood, Swedish Warmblood, Oldenburg*, and the *Irish Sport Horse*.

*Mules* have very independent personalities and often demand more than beginners can give, but they are loyal partners when they decide you are worthy of them. *Mustangs* available through BLM adoptions are wild and need a great deal of time and training to be safe rides, particularly for novices.

People with aching joints or mobility issues find that gaited horses are often a good option. *Paso Fino* horses are unique because they move laterally—left legs together, right legs together. This gives them a smooth motion that is very comfortable to sit because there is no bouncing. Other gaited breeds with smooth movement include the *Saddlebred, Icelandic ponies, Tennessee Walking Horse, Kentucky Walking Horse*, and *Missouri Fox Trotter*.

## BUY OR LEASE?

Once you are thoroughly addicted to riding, you naturally start thinking about owning your own steed. You like the school horse you're riding, but you're a little jealous of the riders who have their own equine partners with their barn nicknames, nameplates on the stall door, and monogrammed saddle pads. Forget binge-watching the latest hit on Hulu; your new addiction is browsing dreamhorse.com.

While having a horse to call your own is everyone's dream, sometimes that's not practical. Horse ownership is a huge responsibility and expense. And if you decide it's not working out, you quickly learn that selling a horse is never easy. You rarely get back in the purchase price what you have paid in board, feed, lessons, and emotional investment. There are other financial considerations. When you retire your horse, are you able to pay for a pasture ornament that you can no longer ride? That's hard enough when the horse is older, and retirement was expected. It's more complicated when the horse is young and the retirement results from injury or illness. Even more so if that means you cannot afford another horse, doubly so if the retired horse will likely survive another 10 or more years.

If you haven't totally committed to a horse-centric lifestyle or think that other situations might interfere, consider leasing. It's a good way to experience the obligations of horse ownership without a long-term commitment.

You'll often find parents wanting to lease a horse when their child is headed off to college and they don't want to foot the bill for the horse; when someone's schedule doesn't allow her to ride as often as she wants, or she doesn't want to sell her horse, but her economic situation is dire. You can occasionally find someone who is willing to let you lease her horse for a trial period before deciding on buying.

With a lease, you share the horse with his owner. There are several variations of the arrangement.

"Full lease/free lease" means it's essentially your horse. You pick up all the costs, including board, farrier, dentist, vet, and more, but you do not own him. If the owner decides to sell the horse or cancel the lease, you lose everything you've paid.

"Half lease" means the two of you split the costs. You can both use the horse, which means agreeing on schedules, showing, and other details. Again, if the lease ends, you lose your money.

"Part lease" means you and the owner agree on how often you can ride the horse. You pay either a flat fee or by the ride. Usually, you pay few, if any, of the other bills.

The biggest advantage of leasing is that if you decide a particular horse isn't a good match or that horse ownership is not for you, you are not left trying to sell or rehome a horse and paying the bills until you can. If finances take a nosedive, you are protected from having to pay more bills. The biggest disadvantage is that when the lease ends, you have nothing to show for the money you've spent but good memories.

If you decide to lease a horse, get everything in writing. A written contract guarantees there are no misunderstandings. People often agree on a lease verbally and with a handshake. They may have great intentions, but later discover that each person thought different things were included or understood the agreement differently. This can turn very unpleasant very quickly, especially in the area of vet bills and unexpected expenses. Do an online search for "sample horse lease agreements" (some examples can be found on www.ridersofacertainage.com). Ask barn owners and other riders with leasing experience to show you what they use.

## HOW AND WHERE TO LOOK (FIND A MENTOR!)

The most important bit of advice for horse-shoppers is this: don't look on your own, particularly if you have no experience in horse dealing. Even experienced, knowledgeable horsewomen tell tales about being taken in and buying an unsuitable horse. As a novice, you are a prime candidate for scams that make the "We have a fortune waiting for you" emails look legitimate. Because of preconceptions about women in general and those in our age group specifically, less-than-ethical dealers and sellers often consider us to be naïve dilettantes with extra cash and no common sense. They might try to fob off an unsuitable horse or sell you a perfect mount but with a much higher price tag than it is worth.

Your instructor is the best person to help you with your search. In fact, many instructors and trainers regularly "horse shop" for clients for a commission—so certainly don't expect her to do it for free. If she thinks the lesson horse you are riding is right for you and she is interested in selling, good. She might have another horse in the stable that is also suitable. More than likely, she wants to keep her lesson horses since a good lesson horse is hard to find. Since she is tied into the local horse community, she knows who has horses available, which sellers are reputable, and which ones to avoid.

If you are looking on your own, seek out a trusted advisor with experience. Tell people in the local equine community that you are shopping. As a courtesy, let everyone who is helping you know that you are asking others to help. As with your instructor, a person selling a horse often gives the person who connects her to a buyer a share of the selling price. It's awkward, at best, if two different people send you to the same seller.

If you can't find a suitable horse locally, expand your search. Online sites post descriptions, photos, often videos, location, and prices. Copy the URLs of the horses that appeal to you. Make copies of posters you see at the feed store and highlight ads in the local horse magazines and the classifieds in club newsletters. Share them with your horse hunt advisor. Don't be surprised if she rejects every one of them, particularly if she has been in the horse business for a long time. She should give you a reason why she's unimpressed. Usually, the description is too glowing to be accurate, the photos or video show some fault you didn't recognize, or the price is out of line for the horse's age and activity. It's a good learning experience for you. After a while, you'll start to understand the language of the ads and translate the descriptions with a proper amount of skepticism.

If you and your advisor find a likely prospect, have her call the seller for a long conversation. She will know what questions to ask and can figure out what is being sold versus what the ads say. The language of horse trading is complicated and full of shades of meaning that are often misleading.

If that conversation goes well, schedule a visit with the two of you. Let your advisor take the lead. She knows what you want, what you need, what you can handle, and what you can spend. Sadly, the stereotype of the smiling, friendly, apparently sincere horse trader who turns out to be a skilled con artist is all too accurate, especially when he is dealing with a novice buyer. He knows how to play on your eagerness to have a horse and can maneuver you into ignoring your advisor or your own internal alarm system.

## *Evaluating a Potential Horse*

➤ When you arrive at the barn, spend some time with the horse. Is he friendly? Does he have good barn manners?

➤ Ask to groom him. Pick up his feet and clean his hoofs. Lead him around. Are you comfortable with him?

➤ Watch him be saddled. If he is already saddled, ask if he can be untacked and resaddled while you watch. Even better, saddle him yourself.

➤ The owner will probably ride the horse. Fair enough. She wants to show him off. But she doesn't know how you ride. You need to get on and see if the two of you click. If the seller is reluctant to let you ride or makes excuses about anything the horse does, that's a red flag.

➤ Your advisor should hop on before you. With her experience, she will feel whether this horse is a good candidate for you. She might also detect things about the horse you might miss.

➤ Are you comfortable riding him? The saddle might not fit you well, but you should be able to tell if any discomfort is more than that.

➤ Does the seller have to offer advice to help the two of you get along? Is that just a "getting to know you" comment, or is it a possible heads-up for a behavior issue or idiosyncrasy you need to know?

➤ Does the horse accept you? Does he respond to your aids or requests?

➤ Do you feel safe? It's normal to be nervous on a horse you don't know, but do you still feel that way after 10 minutes?

➤ If possible, video your ride. It's good for you and your advisor to review it together and discuss the good and bad points of the ride and the horse.

Sellers often complain about bad behavior and attitudes of buyers. Just as there are qualities of good instructors, good buyers share certain traits. Show up for your appointment on time. The seller is rearranging her schedule, which can be inconvenient, especially if your visit is on a weekend and the seller is an instructor with a full day of lessons planned. Be serious about buying. Window shopping just to see what's available or trying horses that are outside your budget is rude. Bring your advisor and be dressed and ready to ride. If you go far enough in negotiations to schedule a pre-purchase exam (see p. 130), the seller will probably discourage other potential buyers. Backing out of the sale before the exam (or after the exam if the horse passes) will cause hard feelings unless there is an overriding reason for doing so.

If all goes well, ask to see the veterinary records; find out what kind of keeper he is and his feeding program. Ask how he gets along with other horses, his barn manners, and his personality. Again, your advisor can translate what the seller is saying into what that really means. If the horse is at a boarding facility, chat with other riders at the barn and get their impression of the horse. Adults might be diplomatic so be sure to say "Hi" to the barn rats. Kids are often more candid. If they love the horse, chances are you will, too.

## WHERE ELSE TO LOOK: ADOPTIONS, SALE BARNS, AND AUCTIONS

Rescue organizations often have lovely horses available for adoption. Most horses at rescues or in rehoming programs are there because their former owners were aging, moving, or facing medical issues. However, there is the perception that horses available for adoption were seized in abuse or neglect cases or have behavioral or physical problems that make them unsuitable as riding or companion horses.

Industry and equine welfare groups are working hard to change that erroneous perception and make finding and adopting good horses easier. The United Horse Coalition works to educate the horse industry about the issues facing horses at risk. Part of the American Horse Council, the Coalition provides information and support for existing and prospective horse owners, breeders, sellers, and horse organizations about owning and caring for horses. Dovetailing with that, the ASPCA operates The Right Horse Initiative, an online directory of horses available for adoption nationwide. There's a complete profile of each horse's history, behavior, and any medical issues. The emphasis is ensuring that every adoption is a good match and successful.

A legitimate horse rescue will be a registered 501(c)(3) charity or a municipal shelter run by a local government agency. If it is not, beware. A legitimate rescue puts time and money into restoring the health of the horses in their care and retraining them for the style of riding that is best for them. The rescue often knows the horse's history and will be honest about any physical and personality issues. Many organizations require that you ride and train with them several times under their supervision to ensure you are a good match. They will check that you have the knowledge and facilities to care for the horse properly. They also agree to take the horse back if the adoption is unsuccessful or the adopter cannot continue to care for the horse. The adoption fee is reasonable and compensates the agency for the board, training, vet bills, and operating expenses.

While there are honest, sincere individuals who take in and rehome horses, private rescues often do not have the experience to provide the best care or training for a rescued animal. While you could come home with a dream horse that just needed a safe place to land, you could also purchase a horse with a litany of problems and expenses. As with the registered charities we've already discussed, any individual rescue should have details and information about the horse. They should also charge a fair fee, strive to ensure that it's a good match, and provide a means of returning the horse if it doesn't work out.

Sadly, there are rescue scams that take advantage of unsavvy prospective buyers. They'll spin you a story about saving the horse from a dire situation and tell you that they've spent hundreds, if not thousands, of dollars on vet and farrier bills and months of training. You pay a high adoption fee only to get home and discover the horse has health problems or no training. And the seller will rarely, if ever, take the horse back. If an individual rescue balks at giving you verifiable details about the horse's background, letting you ride the horse, or performing a pre-purchase exam, be very cautious and consider looking elsewhere.

Sale barns are another option. They buy and sell horses on consignment. For many owners, it is much easier to arrange for a professional to sell their horses than to deal with advertising, scheduling meetings, negotiating prices, and arranging shipment. Many riding schools, trail ride operations, and summer camps with riding programs rely on sale barns for their horses. Because those clients need quiet, dependable horses, the sale barns look for mounts that are safe for inexperienced riders. The reputable barns welcome vet exams and provide medical records, allow test rides, and have some sort of return policy. Those that work with summer camps and trail ride operations often have sales in the late summer and autumn as those operations shut down for the winter.

Another option is getting a horse from an auction. If you do your homework, an auction can be an excellent place to find a good horse. Terminology can be a bit confusing here. Sale barns may also have auctions. Sometimes a business calls itself a sale barn but is primarily an auction house. Find out as much as you can about the facility before you visit. Auction houses may not have the same interest in individual sales as a dedicated sale barn. There may not be the same concern about knowing a horse's history and rideability. Go to the auction with a knowledgeable horseperson. Look over the horses, talk to the management and people selling the horses, find out as much about the horse you are interested in as you can. Some auctions have veterinarians on-site to give exams; some don't. Some allow returns within a short time frame; at other auctions, the horse is sold "as is." Some allow a test ride, but many places don't have the space or time to offer that.

Attending a horse auction is an emotionally draining experience. It's impossible to go to an auction and not want to buy every horse that you see. There are many wonderful horses begging to come home with you, but it's another case of buyer beware. Auctioneers are professionals who can read your body language. You can fall victim to "auction fever" and bid far more than you planned or what the horse is worth. Go with your experienced advisor and pay attention to her evaluation. Weigh your heartstrings against the time, effort, and money you'll invest in an unknown.

### Kill Pens

This is a complicated situation in which doing the right thing individually promotes a larger wrong.

Horse slaughter has been banned in the United States since 2005, with the last slaughterhouse closing in 2007. However, it is legal to ship horses out of the country to be slaughtered for human consumption. Horses are flown to Japan and shipped by truck to Mexico and Canada. Laws banning this have been proposed, but at the time of writing, the practice is still legal.

This situation has led to "kill buying." Slaughterhouses contract with buyers to deliver a quota of horses. The buyers attend auctions to purchase horses. Often these are old and sick horses that have been denied a compassionate death. Since these are horses that would not be purchased otherwise, the buyers pay only a "price per pound" for the horse, which is usually far less than a dollar a pound. Others are apparently sound horses that they purchased for low bids.

All the horses are held in a corral, or "kill pen," as the buyer waits for the transport truck. During this time, the buyer is happy to sell you one of the horses. As with any other purchase, it is a gamble whether you are buying a horse that needs love, feed, and proper turnout, or a horse that went to auction because of health or behavioral problems. You won't be able to perform a pre-purchase exam, and there are probably no valid papers or information about the horse.

Kill buyers will charge a higher price than what they paid and much more than what they will get at the slaughterhouse. And while you may have saved the horse that you purchased, the kill buyer takes that profit and just buys more horses for transport.

There is another scheme run by kill buyers. They post a photo of a horse online with a claim that if it is not saved by donations, it will be shipped to slaughter. The "bail" is significantly higher than what the horse would cost if sold ethically. As with buying a horse from a kill pen, the profit from this sale goes to purchase more horses for slaughter.

There's a misconception that if enough people buy "kill pen" horses, there won't be enough horses to ship for slaughter, and the industry will collapse. Sadly, that is not true. The buyer will meet his quota. Unwanted horses are always available.

In the end, this is a situation in which saving one horse inadvertently leads to a sad ending for others. The problem won't end until legislation banning the shipment of horses for slaughter is passed.

## THE PRE-PURCHASE EXAM (AKA THE VET CHECK)

Whether you are buying, leasing, or adopting, one of the most important things you must do is have a veterinarian perform a pre-purchase inspection. Even if you are purchasing a horse from the stable where you ride, even if it is the horse you regularly ride, insist on a pre-purchase exam. This should detect any physical issues that might require medical treatment, stall rest, or other complications in the future. In the case of a lease, the exam protects you from getting caught in a situation where you pay bills while you can't ride the horse. Never have an inspection done by the owner's veterinarian. There is too much of a chance of a conflict of interest for the veterinarian. If the owner does not want you to use the veterinarian of your choice, be suspicious.

The veterinarian will give the horse a thorough medical check-up with X-rays, a review of vaccinations, dental work, past medical care, lameness issues, blood work, and exams for other known and possible conditions. Ask about testing for conditions and diseases common in your geographic location, like Lyme Disease spread by ticks and EPM (Equine Protozoal Myeloencephalitis) spread by possums. Some of the blood will be held for several weeks. That's because less-than-honest sellers sometimes drug the horse to cover a physical or behavioral issue. If you get the horse home and problems appear, the veterinarian can run blood tests to determine if the horse was sedated or medicated. The veterinarian will give you a detailed report on the examination, including the results of any blood tests. Copies of the radiographs (X-rays) will be available through the vet's practice or an online medical records system.

If asked, a veterinarian can do a superficial inspection and only check for significant problems. This usually happens when you already know the horse and owner and you both think you know the horse's health. You run the risk, though, of the horse not yet showing symptoms of a condition. You could buy the horse, but six months later, he develops something that could have been detected with a more extensive vet check. It is expensive to have a thorough pre-purchase examination, but consider what it might cost to treat a condition you could have seen or known about if you hadn't skimped—not to mention the loss suffered when you are unable to ride but still paying board, veterinary, and other bills.

A thorough veterinary exam points out things that may be minor but must be considered. For some veterinarians, too many negatives, even minor ones, will cause them to recommend against buying or leasing the horse. This is a sensible comment because the veterinarian is representing your interests. However, every horse has some defects.

Balance your goals with the health of the horse. For example, most horses in their later teens will show some arthritis. This can be a red flag. But many older horses are like us older riders—a bit stiff in the mornings. A dose of an anti-inflammatory and a warm-up may be all he needs, especially if you are primarily trail riding, doing low-level dressage, and trotting over 18-inch cross-rails.

If you want to ride Prix St. George, take on an intermediate cross-country course, or participate in endurance competitions, however, the demands can severely aggravate the condition. Similarly, a history of hoof problems, colic, or other chronic issues may be warnings to look for another horse, no matter how deeply you have fallen in love with this one.

## SIGNING THE PAPERWORK

Finally, all the questions are answered; all that's left is signing the paperwork. Once again, you need a contract. Most professional barns and horse dealers have a standard sales contract. Do not buy a horse without a contract, even when you are buying from a friend. The contract is the only proof you have that you are the horse's legal owner. (Links to sample sales contracts are on www.ridersofacertainage.com.)

Beyond the general terms of sale, some contracts include many additional clauses and stipulations. Some give the seller first rights to buy back the horse if you decide to sell it in the future. Others limit to whom and under what circumstances you can sell the horse. Some contracts stipulate what kind of riding you can do, including whether you can show the horse or ride it in specific disciplines and conditions. These may seem unfair since you now own the horse, but it usually indicates that the seller is looking out for the horse's best interest. The seller may not know you, and she wants to guarantee that the horse will be well cared for and that you are not going to misuse him or sell him to the knackers.

Now he's yours. Congratulations! You can rename him, dress him up, and start paying the bills. At parties, you can share stories with other horse people about all his idiosyncrasies while the non-horse people drift away from you. And you will soon learn the first rule of horse ownership—the cheapest thing about owning a horse is the cost of buying him.

CHAPTER 15

# Boarding:
# Finding a Home for Your Horse

## TYPES OF BOARD

There are different types of board. Boarding prices depend on the size of the operation and the facilities. A small farm with the owners caring for a couple of horses will charge a lot less than a full-service stable with an indoor arena and a riding program. As the saying goes, "You get what you pay for."

"Full board" generally means that your horse receives feed, hay, turnout to pasture, and seasonal care—like blanketing in winter and in a stall with a fan during the day in the summer. The staff mucks out the stall. You pay for supplements, farrier, dentist, and vet services. Often, the stable will charge you a fee if one of the staff must be on hand to handle your horse for professional services, like holding him for the farrier, administering medications, monitoring saddle fit, or deworming. Ask lots of questions so that you know exactly what you get for your board fee.

"Field board/pasture board/self-board" can be compared to the stable being an equine parking lot. It's a lot like keeping the horse on your own property. Your monthly

# *Good Boarder Guidelines*

There is more to being a good boarder than paying your board bill on time (although that will endear you to the owner). Much of it is attitude and common sense, and it is similar to the qualities I discussed when it comes to being a good riding student at a lesson barn.

➤ Behave with a respectful, polite attitude toward the owners, instructors, and other students.

➤ Avoid gossip and drama.

➤ Take problems to the management instead of complaining in the barn aisle.

➤ Don't give treats to other people's horses, use other people's equipment, or ride someone else's horse without permission.

➤ Be considerate when sharing riding arenas or other facilities. Don't use more space than you need and appreciate that other people's horses may need more time and space than yours.

➤ Clean up after yourself and keep the wash rack, tack room, and other common areas tidy.

➤ Respect the owner's experience and do not tell her how to run her business. Appreciate the costs of running a stable and the time, energy, and work that are involved.

➤ Remember that the barn manager has a life away from the barn. Save messaging and phone calls for work hours unless it is an emergency.

➤ If there are barn opening hours, respect those.

➤ Offer to help when you can. Help fix fences or move the round pen, pick up a brush and do the little painting jobs that the owner never has time to do. Help organize riding camps. Buy little things that make life easier for the staff, like a timer for the water hose or a shower wand for the wash rack. Occasionally fill the fridge with water (or wine coolers).

fee buys you a space in the fields and sometimes a stall in the barn. You are responsible for providing your own grain, supplements, wormers, and hay, also for feeding your horse. You provide your own bedding, and if you have a stall, you muck it out.

While the cost of do-it-yourself board appears to be cheaper than full board, add up the other expenses and your time factor before deciding if this is truly a benefit and a bargain. Spending time with your horse every day certainly builds a stronger bond between the two of you, but the most common complaint of people who keep their horses at home or who use a self-care boarding arrangement is that they are so busy with their chores that they have no time to ride.

If the financial savings of self-care are the only way to afford a horse, ask yourself if you should do so. If your finances are that tight, you probably don't have a reserve for emergencies, like an unexpected vet bill, a lost job, a major car repair, or hay prices that skyrocket because of drought or flooding. Leasing or taking lessons on a school horse may be a better option.

Always get a written contract for all boarding situations. Never enter a boarding situation without spelling out everything in writing. Verbal agreements, even those made with the best intentions, are "worth the paper they are written on," which is nothing at all. If the barn you are considering does not have a boarding contract, get contracts from other barns, or look for examples online and use them. Even if you plan to board at a friend's farm, insist that you have a contract. It protects both of you from misunderstandings that can end a friendship. (Links to sample boarding contracts are at www.ridersofacertainage.com.)

Some stables operate as "co-ops." Members share the cost of maintenance, utility bills, and pasture management (mowing and fertilizing), and sometimes the cost of the property rental and the mortgage. They chip in to pay for hoses, muck buckets, and fencing. Depending on the co-op, members share the cost of feed and hay. In others, hay is a communal cost, but feed and supplements are the responsibility of each owner. They often use the same farrier, vet, and dentist and coordinate schedules to split the cost of barn calls. There's a schedule for taking turns feeding, filling water buckets, and cleaning troughs, and agreed-upon procedures for mucking stalls, turnout, blanketing, and keeping the wash stall tidy.

The track record for co-ops is uneven. They work best when they involve just a few people who share the same ideas about standards of care and "horsekeeping." The members regularly check in with each other, flag any problems, and work out disagreements.

Co-ops fail when the agreements are forgotten or ignored. This is particularly true when the agreements were only oral. Most commonly, members complain that

## AGELESS ADVICE

## *Boarding Facility Checklist*

These are some of the most important things to know about a barn. You are paying a substantial fee to the stable. You need to know as much about the place as you can. A reputable barn owner will be glad to answer your questions.

➤ Is the barn clean and well-maintained?

➤ Are the people on staff competent? Do they have experience? Is the barn manager supervising them well?

➤ Does the barn manager have a thorough grounding in nutrition and horse care, or are you responsible for developing a feeding and supplement program?

➤ What is the turnout schedule? Is it adjusted for seasonal conditions?

➤ How are new horses introduced to the herd? Are there options if horses do not get along?

➤ Are the fields in good condition? What is the quality of the pasture forage? Is there a pasture management plan?

➤ Can the field handle weather changes? For example, is there good drainage, or will the field become a swamp or flood in periods of rain or the spring thaw?

chores aren't done or are done poorly, feed isn't weighed properly, or supplements aren't given. Some members are uncomfortable or unable to handle the horses of other co-op members. Tempers start to fray, and the atmosphere becomes testy. Often, people move their horses to another barn.

## EVALUATING A BOARDING BARN

Hand in hand with finding the perfect horse is finding the perfect place to keep him. If you have your own farm, this is not an issue. But if you don't, you need to

### AGELESS ADVICE

➤ Is there shelter, a windbreak, run-in sheds?

➤ Is there adequate water in the fields? Are there automatic waterers or water troughs?

➤ If there are water troughs, are they cleaned regularly? If the farm depends on well water, what happens in a drought?

➤ Can you choose your own vets, farriers, dentists, and other professionals?

➤ Are riding areas regularly available? Is there a lot of competition to use the arena or training areas? Are there other areas to ride if the arena is in use?

➤ Do you feel as though you can discuss problems and ask the management questions?

➤ If the stable has a resident instructor, you probably cannot use anyone else, but there is no harm in asking. If there is no designated instructor, what are the rules and limitations on bringing in someone? Usually, the instructor must prove she has liability insurance. If it is a competition barn, there may be a conflict of interest if she also instructs at rival facilities.

find proper boarding. Even if you have your own acreage, boarding is often attractive to older women, particularly if they live alone or their experience with horses is limited.

Location, facilities, and price are the primary considerations. But there are many other things to consider, some of which are not so obvious. You may find that the best barn for you and your horse is neither the closest nor the cheapest.

CHAPTER 16

# But Wait! There's More!
# Your Professional Support Team

In addition to the obvious expenses of board and feed, many costs are often forgotten in the excitement of horse shopping. You overlook them because you don't encounter them daily or you haven't priced them out. The cadre of professionals you rely on is vital for the health, safety, and comfort of your horse and you.

## VETERINARIAN

Veterinarians never have a slow season, but they stay particularly busy in spring and fall when they make the rounds of their clients to administer vaccines. If you are very lucky, that's the only time you will see yours.

Your horse needs an annual check-up. This can be done when the veterinarian comes to give routine vaccinations. There are other times when you need to see your veterinarian for non-emergencies. You need a health certificate whenever you travel out of state. Depending on where you live and where you are going, the certificate is valid for between 30 to 90 days. In addition, insurance companies require a health certificate and evaluation for equine medical insurance.

Learn the normal vital signs of horses. Ask your vet or instructor to show you how to take your horse's pulse and temperature, measure his respiration, listen for gut noises, perform the "pinch test" to check for dehydration, and check the capillaries for proper blood flow. Record all this on a chart and keep it someplace handy in your tack box and barn. (Links to online videos that demonstrate how to take vital signs and the forms to record them are at www.ridersofacertainage.com.)

Read up on common equine problems, like colic and abscesses. Learn their symptoms, how to care for them, and when to call the vet. Buy a book on equine first aid; take a course if you can. Keep a well-stocked first aid kit at the barn and know how to use it.

Don't be afraid to call your veterinarian when something doesn't seem right. Most veterinarians would rather answer questions or make a barn call for something that turns out to be minor than have you think you are overreacting, not call, and the situation turns out to be serious.

When you call, have the horse's current vital signs ready. Thanks to the wonders of technology, you can take a photo or video of an injured or sick horse and send it to your veterinarian via messaging or email. It can help the veterinarian determine what you need to do before—or instead of—scheduling an appointment. Finally, while internet chat groups are wonderful places to discuss your favorite ride and antics of your horse, these are not the places to look for veterinary advice. Veterinarians run some internet groups, but a live discussion with the veterinarian who knows you and your horse is always better.

Veterinarians charge a fee for the farm visit, which can be a bit expensive when you don't live near the vet's office. For routine situations, like vaccinations or the annual exam, ask if you can trailer your horse to another nearby stable (with that stable's permission) or have people bring their horses to yours. That way, everyone splits the travel fee. Many vets are agreeable to this; it makes their life easier by saving them driving time.

## *Emergency Calls*

Some situations demand you contact your veterinarian immediately:

➤ A broken limb.

➤ Colic. Learn the symptoms—they can develop very quickly and dramatically or be quite subtle.

➤ Choke. This happens when food gets caught in the horse's esophagus. It generally does not block the breathing passages, so you don't need to learn an equine Heimlich maneuver, but the horse cannot drink or swallow until the obstruction is removed.

➤ Heavy bleeding from an injury.

➤ A foreign object protruding from the horse. (Do not remove it.)

➤ Injury or wound near eyes, tendons, or genitals.

➤ Any issue concerning the eye—can't open it, cut on eyelid, pus or discharge.

➤ Severe lameness or unsoundness—the horse can't put weight on the limb.

➤ Staggering or other signs of lack of coordination or confusion.

➤ Excessive, continuous, watery diarrhea.

➤ Fever.

➤ Rapid pulse at rest.

➤ Rapid breathing at rest.

➤ Heatstroke.

➤ Multiple animals showing the same symptoms.

➤ Pregnant mare not delivering after 20 minutes of labor.

### Vaccinations and Tests

Vaccines work by stimulating the immune system to produce antibodies that combat a specific bacterial disease or virus. Should the bacteria or virus appear later, the antibodies are primed to kick in and kill the infection.

There are conflicting views about the need for giving vaccines as often as is currently recommended. Some studies indicate that the core vaccines (East/West equine encephalitis, rabies, tetanus, and West Nile) administered and boosted correctly when the animal is young, provide life-long protection, and that annual boosters may not be necessary. Instead of regular boosters, some veterinarians recommend titer tests. These tests measure the level of antibodies in the blood. When the titers are high for specific bacteria or a virus, there may be no need for revaccination. There is a lot of debate about whether this is a valid indicator of protection. The American Veterinary Medical Association says the data are unclear.

A combination vaccine can contain as many as six different antigens, which is

---

**AGELESS ADVICE**

## *Core Vaccines*

The American Association of Equine Practitioners (AAEP) recommends several core vaccinations. These are the immunizations or vaccines they consider the most essential for every horse:

➤ *Annual:* East/West equine encephalitis (a form of sleeping sickness that is almost always fatal), rabies, tetanus, West Nile virus, strangles

➤ *Semi-annual:* Rhinoneumosis/Herpesvirus (often shortened to "rhino"), influenza.

➤ *Occasional:* Administered depending on the situation and geographic location. Your veterinarian will recommend the appropriate vaccines.

more comfortable for the horse than several individual injections. The combination may slightly increase the chances of an adverse reaction, but advanced techniques for preparing vaccines have largely eliminated that concern. A few vaccines can be given intranasally by drops in the nose. These are easier to administer and have few side effects.

Discuss vaccine options with your veterinarian. She will have the most current information on studies, new versions of vaccines, and the most valid recommendations. The decisions should consider risk factors like the effectiveness of any vaccine and the potential adverse reactions; whether your horse is farm-based or traveling; if other horses come to the farm, either to stay for training or trailering in and out for a lesson; the age of the horse; and environmental factors like the mosquito population.

The primary annual test performed on horses is the Coggins test. Not a vaccination, the Coggins test determines if your horse has been exposed to Equine Infectious Anemia (EIA). This is a highly infectious virus that can be fatal to horses, mules, or donkeys. It is spread by biting insects like the horsefly. Some horses that carry the virus show no symptoms and will always remain contagious. They must be strictly quarantined and kept at least 200 yards from any other horse for the rest of their lives. Because there are very few facilities that can manage such requirements, the horse is usually euthanized.

To perform a Coggins test, the veterinarian draws blood and sends it to a state-run laboratory. Results come back in about a week. You receive a certificate or, more frequently, directions to an online veterinarian records portal where the results are kept on file and can be printed out.

Because EIA is so contagious and potentially devastating, health officials are very strict about identifying and controlling it. Most stables and horse shows require proof of a negative Coggins test to stay there or participate in activities. Many places will not allow you to remove your horse from the trailer until you have presented a negative Coggins test.

A negative Coggins is required to cross state lines with your horse. Some states require you to stop at an agricultural checkpoint and produce a health certificate for your horse, which includes the negative Coggins plus a record of vaccinations and proof of the horse's physical condition when it began the trip.

### Deworming

Worms—intestinal parasites—live in your horse's gut. They serve no known purpose. All horses have a colony of at least one type of worm setting up housekeeping inside them. It is important to keep the population low because the parasites can cause health problems like weight loss, diarrhea, colic, ulcers, skin sores, disrupted gut function, and itchy butt.

Worm infestation is a "chicken-and-egg" situation. It starts when your horse eats egg-or-larva-infested grass. The eggs develop in the gut, and the newly hatched larvae and undeveloped eggs pass out of the horse in his manure. They are now back in the environment where the horse eats the infested grass, and the cycle begins again.

Traditionally, horses were dewormed every 12 weeks using three different chemicals administered in rotation. Dewormers are in a tube of paste that is injected into the (often uncooperative) horse's mouth. However, worms are developing a resistance to the chemicals and are harder to kill. Evidence now shows a possible correlation between routine deworming and colic, with enough horses developing colic within a few days of deworming to cause concern. Consequently, a new strategy is to develop a deworming program for individual horses. This is done by fecal egg count. The manure from a horse is examined to determine the level of the worm population. Even horses pastured in the same field and eating the same grass can have very different levels of worm infestation. Dewormer is administered according to the level of infestation. Your veterinarian can make the best recommendation for a deworming schedule.

## FARRIER

"No hoof, no horse." Your farrier plays a critical role in keeping your horse healthy. On average, your horse needs a pedicure every four to eight weeks. It depends on how fast your horse's feet grow. During the winter, hooves grow more slowly; in summer, the growth speeds up. In general, it takes between 9 to 12 months for a hoof to grow from the coronary band to the ground.

The mystery of horses' feet and legs is a growing field of study, high-end research, and continuing education for farriers. Riding clubs and county extension services occasionally offer programs for horse owners that teach the basics of foot mechanics, anatomy, and care. If you have a chance, take one of them. You'll have a better understanding of your farrier's role in your horse's health.

Your farrier should be willing to explain what she is doing and why. Most farriers appreciate clients who want to understand their horse's needs and who recognize and respect the farrier's experience.

Farriers begin their professional careers by attending a course that lasts between two and three months. They learn foot and leg anatomy, conformation, hoof diseases, handling horses, reading X-rays, blacksmithing skills, corrective shoeing, and business skills. Some programs include an apprenticeship under the supervision of an experienced farrier.

There is no licensing requirement for farriers, but there are several professional associations. Many farriers who do not belong to any association are excellent professionals who independently keep up with trends and research. Be more concerned with the job they do than with the membership cards.

There's an ongoing, often heated debate about whether horses should be shod or go "barefoot." You need to discuss this with your farrier before making a decision. It depends on your horse, his conformation, hoof health, the kind of riding you do, and the type of ground you ride on. The arguments for and against shoeing are well-presented in magazines and online, but your farrier is the person who knows your horse and his hooves better than anyone else.

Farriers have an unfortunate reputation for showing up late, which inevitably happens on the day you are on a tight schedule yourself. That's the nature of their job. They are generally covering many miles, crisscrossing the area to serve their clients. They plan their time based on how long they expect any job to take and how long it takes them to travel between stables. All it takes to throw off the schedule is one usually cooperative horse deciding to be difficult, a traffic tie-up, or an emergency call that can't wait. Be patient and understanding when things go haywire. It's not deliberate. Most farriers try to call if they are tied up and either revise their ETA or reschedule. If you are a good client and work with your farrier's situation, she'll put you on the top of the list for preferential treatment.

Farrier's fees vary greatly even within the same geographic area. They depend on what needs to be done and the reputation of the farrier. Someone whose client list includes high-end stables and show horses may well charge more than someone who has less experience or works primarily with recreational riders. As always, ask around for recommendations, and feel free to try several farriers before making a final decision. When you find a good farrier—patient with your horse (and you), generally on time, happy to educate you—treat that person like gold. Have cold drinks in the summer, plates of cookies and a gift card for birthdays and Christmas (gasoline gift cards are particularly welcome). And praise her to your friends. Referrals are important to the farriery business.

## DENTIST

Horses' teeth never stop growing. This is not a problem in the wild because constant grazing on often tough grasses in poor soil keeps the teeth ground down. Domesticated horses, however, must have their teeth filed down, a process known as "floating."

At one time, a veterinarian or dentist would show up with a metal rasp, crank the horse's mouth open, and file away. Later, the use of Dremel drills sped up the process, but the operators worked without much understanding of what they were doing. They only knew that the teeth needed to be filed down.

Like farrier work, the field of equine dentistry is now much more sophisticated. Dentists still use rasps and drills but with a far greater understanding of how to properly manage a horse's dental needs. Equine dentists now attend schools where they learn the anatomy of a horse's mouth, common illnesses and treatments, radiography, and other conditions that affect oral health.

Opinions vary as to how often teeth need to be floated: every six months, nine months, or once a year. Your dentist will have an opinion based on the specific needs of your horse. If your horse is refusing to take the bit, is fussy about his head, or is not eating well, a call to your dentist may be in order. Routine care includes filing down hooks on teeth that can cause a horse to bite his own cheek or have trouble chewing, removing "wolf teeth," which are small, unnecessary teeth that can interfere with the bit, and other minor needs.

Usually, horses must be sedated for dental work, especially when power equipment is involved. Quite understandably, your horse doesn't appreciate having a large, hinged metal speculum shoved into his mouth and cranked open, much less enjoy the rasping and drilling or having a tooth extracted. Unless the dentist is also a veterinarian, you must arrange for a veterinarian to be on hand to administer sedation. Often, you can coordinate the dentist's visit with the veterinarian's regular checkup visit, vaccine schedule, or some other reason to be at the stable.

The cost of dental work depends on what needs to be done. The fee generally does not include the cost of the sedative, which is charged by the veterinarian, or the fee for travel to the stable (the barn call). If more than one horse needs dental care, the owners split the barn call fee. Often local horse owners agree to haul their horses to one barn, so the dentist does not have to travel to different farms, which further reduces the barn fee and makes the day easier for the dentist and vet.

## SADDLE FITTER

Riding shouldn't hurt—either you or your horse! Your horse's reactions while under saddle are a good indication of how well it provides proper and comfortable support for both of you. When riders complain about a bucking, jigging, cinchy, or tight horse, the first thing to check is saddle fit. A poorly fitting saddle is as painful to a horse as wearing a pair of tight shoes is to us. Left uncorrected, it can also lead to back problems and possibly lameness issues and is often the cause of behavioral problems. When a horse needs 15 to 20 minutes to "settle in" or "warm up," it could be a hint that the saddle is a problem. Working with a professional saddle fitter guarantees that you and your horse will enjoy comfortable, healthy rides.

Like many other aspects of the equestrian world, saddle fitters are not required to have any formal certification. Several schools in the United States teach saddle fitting. In addition to individuals interested in the profession, these courses attract equine bodyworkers, veterinarians, chiropractors, and farriers. The courses cover equine and human anatomy, biomechanics, conformation, dynamic and static saddle fit (the difference between a horse standing still and moving), veterinary issues, types of saddles and their uses, and saddle construction. These courses last from a few weeks to several months. Some require apprenticeships, writing detailed case studies to demonstrate practical understanding of concepts, and hands-on saddle-making experience.

When working with a saddle fitter, ask where she got her training. Many sales representatives for saddle companies bill themselves as saddle fitters. They may be well-schooled in the qualities and features of their brand but often have little in-depth knowledge of the field as taught in professional courses.

Most courses for saddle fitters concentrate exclusively on English saddles, although there are a few schools that cover Western saddle fit. This is mainly because the design and construction of Western saddles are much more standardized than English saddles. There is a limited range of widths, trees, and panels. If you cannot find a saddle fitter experienced with Western tack, a knowledgeable instructor and experienced tack store staff can provide a good fit. In addition, there are many online sources and videos with excellent illustrations and explanations.

Saddles were initially designed for men. When women rode, they rode side-saddle, since riding astride in long skirts was both impractical and "immodest." Besides, the medical consensus at the time was that riding astride would damage our reproductive systems. As women began wearing breeches and riding astride, they used "male" saddles. By and large, we still do. However, as I've mentioned already, the female and male pelvis are shaped differently. This means it is more difficult for women to find a saddle that allows for the rider's proper and comfortable riding position that also fits the horse correctly. While the wide variety of saddles available these days means women can usually find one that allows them to ride well, female-centric saddles designed with a woman's bone structure in mind are not widely available.

Even if a newly purchased saddle fits both your horse and you perfectly, that will change as your horse develops muscle. In most cases with Western saddles, changing the thickness of the saddle pad compensates for the changes in a horse's conformation and development of his muscle tone through conditioning. With English saddles, the padding shifts and compresses during everyday riding as well as changing as the horse develops. These changes require adjusting the saddle and padding. Some veterinarians recommend checking saddle fit three to four times a year. This is particularly true if you ride daily or are involved in a concentrated development and conditioning program. More commonly, riders schedule refitting appointments once or twice a year.

Fees vary depending on the fitter. Most fitters charge a flat fee for an evaluation; some also charge a travel fee. The evaluation fee might include adjustments. Otherwise, you can take the fitter's recommendations for adjustments to have the work done elsewhere. Most fitters work closely with saddle repair shops they know and trust. You can also use the recommendations to shop for a new saddle if yours is not appropriate. Many saddle fitters can recommend appropriate saddle brands for you and return for a follow-up visit to ensure proper fit.

# Insurance and Powers of Attorney: Protecting Yourself and Your Horses

P reparing for the unexpected is the best way to survive it. Overall, equine insurance companies are infinitely easier to deal with than any kind of human health or other insurance company.

## MEDICAL COVERAGE

Medical insurance for your horse is as important as health insurance is for you. Veterinary medical expenses are as frighteningly high as human medical bills, and your veterinarian doesn't have the financial resources to cover her expenses until you can pay. Veterinarians try very hard to develop a payment plan with you, but a few dollars a month for thousands of dollars in bills doesn't work. People often go online to criticize veterinarians who don't treat their animals for free or at what the owner considers a low enough price. That public denigration in what is already a stress-filled career is one reason veterinarians have one of the highest suicide rates of any profession. (A survey by the American Medical Veterinary Association found that veterinarians commit suicide at a rate 2.7 times higher than the general population, with female veterinarians 3.5 times more likely to commit suicide than the general population.)

"Major medical" and "mortality" are the most common kinds of equine insurance. Some horses qualify for "loss of use," but that is generally for special cases like high-end show or performance horses or stallions. Companies often deny coverage for a return of some conditions, particularly lameness issues. Typically, once a horse turns 20, medical and mortality coverage ceases.

Most insurers provide coverage based on what you paid for the horse. This determines the cap for medical reimbursement. In some cases, that coverage increases if the horse has a successful record of showing at recognized competitions.

The costs for equine medical insurance and the coverage vary greatly, so work with an insurance broker to compare coverage and prices. You may easily spend over a thousand dollars a year for coverage with a few hundred dollars of deductible. That's a lot of money but consider that colic surgery costs an average of close to $10,000. What does your veterinarian charge for a set of X-rays, an MRI, or a deep laceration that needs stitches and antibiotics?

Mortality insurance pays compensation when your horse dies. The amount is usually the purchase price of the horse. The insurance company often requires a necropsy (the term for an autopsy for an animal) to determine the cause of death. This is paid out of pocket and can run from several hundred to over a thousand dollars. It must be performed at a state lab or veterinary facility, and you are responsible for transporting the remains to the lab. If the results show that the horse died from a condition that is not covered, you receive no compensation.

## LIABILITY INSURANCE

Liability insurance is a must. In today's litigious society, horses are a magnet for lawsuits. If your horse causes an accident, injures someone, or causes property damage, you stand a good chance of being sued no matter the circumstances. It doesn't matter who is at fault—if anyone. Insurance companies will try to recoup whatever they paid out in damages. Even in states with "inherent risk laws" that warn people about the dangers of riding, even with signed waivers, you are still at risk. Personal injury lawyers and insurance companies will look for some element to invalidate your protection. Fortunately, liability insurance is a bargain. A few hundred dollars a year gives you as much as a million dollars of coverage. Get coverage for all your horses, even the pasture ornaments who never leave the farm.

## PERSONAL PROPERTY COVERAGE

Personal property insurance is another consideration. Make sure your tack and equipment stored at the stable or in your trailer are insured. If you are a boarder, those things are not covered in the boarding contract. That is too much of a liability for the stable in the event of a fire or some other disaster and too much of a temptation for things to "go missing." If you own a trailer, include it on your auto insurance policy.

If you have a homeowner's policy, your gear may be covered for situations like fire, theft, or natural disaster. That's often the case, even if it is stored at the stable or in your trailer and not at your home. Check to see what your policy covers. If you don't have a homeowner's policy, you need a separate property insurance policy that costs several hundred dollars annually. To cover losses due to theft, policies generally require that the equipment be secured in a locked area. A communal tack room used by many people may not be included, even if it is locked when no one is around. Depending on your policy, leaving your gear in a locked horse trailer or in a locker with a built-in lock—not just a tack box with a combination lock attached—may give coverage.

Take photographs of all your gear: saddles, tack, brushes, cleaning supplies, saddle pads, bits, used and stored bridles, even your treats and fly spray. Load them onto a hard drive and put it into your safe deposit box or a secure location at home, or upload them to the Cloud. Save receipts, particularly for expensive things like saddles and custom tack or clothing. Write down the serial numbers of all tack and equipment which have them, especially saddles. That makes it easier to track and claim them if they are stolen. If you ever suffer a catastrophic loss, this documentation will make filing claims a lot easier.

## WHO MAKES DECISIONS IF YOU CANNOT

Besides having insurance to cover the vet bills, you must also provide written permission for caretakers to attend to your horse if you are not available.

The primary document is a Power of Attorney. This designates who can care for your horse if you are not available or cannot make decisions. If you are injured and cannot communicate or can't be contacted in a timely manner for any reason, someone needs the authority to make decisions about your horse. That includes making the call to put the horse down if the situation calls for it.

Find someone you trust who thinks the same way you do about your horse, his care, and his quality of life. This could be your instructor, the stable manager, a riding partner, or your spouse. Another good option is your veterinarian. Have that same conversation and make sure she has the directive that allows her to make decisions independently, if necessary. This is important because your veterinarian can face legal trouble if she performs a procedure or puts your horse down without consulting you first.

It is important to carry a temporary Power of Attorney whenever you travel with your horse. It grants permission to any attending veterinarian to treat your horse when you cannot make decisions. If there is an accident and you are unable to communicate, a veterinarian called to the scene may not be able to treat your horse without that permission. Keep that Power of Attorney and other important papers

(Coggins test results, health certificate, and emergency contacts) in a brightly colored folder and keep the folder in the passenger compartment of your tow vehicle. Have a second folder in the dressing room of your trailer or taped to the door. (Links to both Power of Attorney forms and First Responder information forms are available at www.ridersofacertainage.com.)

## PUTTING YOUR HORSE DOWN

Inevitably, and sadly, there will come a time when you must send your partner over the Rainbow Bridge. One of the hardest decisions you will ever make is calling your veterinarian and making the appointment to put your partner and best friend down. You wonder if it is too soon, if changing his feed or medications will fix the problem, if he will once again spring back from whatever illness or condition affects him. If he is an old horse who's been with you for years, even decades, you recognize that his teeth are gone, he's losing weight, and his arthritis is painful, but he still nickers when he sees you.

While we like to think that our horses will just quietly slip away in their sleep, that is usually not the case. Only one horse in eight dies of natural causes. The others are euthanized either electively or in an emergency. Surveys by the University of Guelph in Toronto show that over 80 percent of horse owners have no plans for end-of-life decisions and state that they don't want to think about it or have to make them.

Often, the heartache at the thought of losing our friend and partner prevents us from considering our horse's best interest. We must base our decision on our horse's quality of life and comfort, not our emotional pain.

Consider those freedoms as you decide what is best for your horse. This decision is all about your horse, not about you. Putting your horse down is not doing it *to* him; you are doing this *for* him. Our horses will often hang on for our sakes. They will endure the pain and weariness because they know we want them to stay,

## The Quality of Life Question

The Canadian National Farm Animal Care Council Code of Practice developed the concept of the Five Freedoms for Quality of Life for animals:

➤ Freedom from hunger and thirst.

➤ Freedom from discomfort.

➤ Freedom from pain, injury, and disease.

➤ Freedom to express natural behavior.

➤ Freedom from fear and distress.

In addition to the Five Freedoms of Quality of Life for Animals, the American Association of Equine Practitioners has its own considerations in making decisions about euthanasia with horses. It states that a horse should not have to endure the following:

➤ Continuous or unmanageable pain from a condition that is chronic and incurable.

➤ A medical condition or surgical procedure that has a poor prognosis for a good quality of life.

➤ Continuous analgesic medication and/or box stall confinement for the relief of pain for the rest of his life.

➤ An unmanageable medical or behavioral condition that renders him a hazard to himself or his handlers.

and they want to please us. Waiting until the bitter end is often very bitter indeed if there is a devastating collapse, a sudden, painful deterioration, and an emergency call to your vet, or your horse is so weak that he can't hang on any longer. As any vet will tell you, it is better to let your horse go "too soon" than to wait even a day too long. And while she will remain cool and professional while she is at the stable, you can bet your vet shares your pain. She knows your horse, too, and that task never becomes routine or easy.

As heartbreaking as it is emotionally, there are practical considerations. Will your horse be put down at the farm or be transported to the veterinarian's office or another location? If he is put down at the farm, what happens to his remains? Many people want to bury the horse on their grounds where he was at home and happy and where you can visit him and feel his presence. In many areas, however, it is illegal to bury a horse over concerns about public health and safety, but often it's a case of, "Don't ask, don't tell." Some locations allow for "composting," where the carcass is covered with a deep layer of wood chips, mulch, sawdust, and straw. Some counties have a crematorium associated with an agriculture department or extension service. If none of those is available, you must find a livestock removal service. Some offer cremation services and will return your horse's ashes. The cost for removal is several hundred dollars and generally must be paid before the remains are removed. These are all preparations you should make long before you call your veterinarian.

Your memories of your partner are not limited to photo portraits of the two of you, pictures from trail rides, and ribbons won at shows. The tradition of clipping the tail as a memento has evolved into a new chance to remember your partner by turning the hair (or ashes if he was cremated) into jewelry. Hair is woven into bracelets, rings, and hatbands. Shadow boxes with your horse's halter and plaster imprint of his hoof hang on your wall. Pendants and lockets hold bits of tail and mane or a small photo. Paperweights and glass sculptures incorporate the horse's ashes into beautiful artwork. The art of placing horsehair into pottery just before it is fired creates uniquely personal pieces. Some people continue to ride with their partner by making mecate reins from his hair. There are many comforting ways of remembering the many happy years and adventures you shared.

# PART SIX

# LIVING WITH
# YOUR HORSE

# CHAPTER 18

# Your Own Place:
# A Home on the Range

## TIME, HEALTH, AND LOCATION

The time has come for you to live your equine dream. You are retiring, and the kids are gone. You have no more daily family or job obligations. Your finances are solid. Your health is fine. It seems that the stars are aligning to make your life-long dream a reality. You can buy a few acres near trails, build a small barn, and keep a few horses. Maybe you'll take in a boarder or two to help cover the bills and to have someone to ride with. You've seen some suitable properties in the area or you're checking out horse-friendly locations all around the country. Soon you'll look out of your kitchen window and sip your morning coffee while watching your furry kids grazing in their field. You'll enjoy spending part of your day grooming and feeding them. It's all very romantic and "*National Velvet*-ish."

Informal surveys show that almost everyone who keeps their horses at home rather than board them has few regrets. The comments also show that the successful "horses at home" people took a hard reality check on the amount of time, energy, physical demands, money, and education involved.

One of the most common disappointing discoveries is that the amount of work needed to care for the horses and barn deeply eats into your actual riding time. If you have a busy life, are still working, or have other off-the-farm demands, maintaining a daily routine can be difficult and exhausting. And while there is no barn drama at your own place, you can also feel quite isolated and lonely. Keeping horses at home can also be more expensive than boarding because you need to purchase equipment and pay for maintenance, cover costs for hay and feed delivery, property insurance, and property taxes. You may have to budget for hired help.

Another issue is health. As we age, our stamina starts slipping, and medical conditions that have always happened to other people now start happening to us. Health problems appear overnight and can be debilitating. At the very least, they can disrupt your regular schedule for a while. Planning must include considering how to adapt to those changes.

Packing up and moving to a new location appeals to many people. Surveys show that almost one-half of the people living in the eastern United States want to move when they retire. They cite a desire for a gentler climate, lower taxes, quality health care, and plentiful cultural opportunities as priorities. Chat groups frequently discuss the best places for horse-oriented retirement or where the employment opportunities are better.

Moving is not a decision to be made lightly. Between our age and the expenses involved, we're not likely to move again if this new place doesn't work out. While people tout their hometown with more enthusiasm than the local Chamber of Commerce, remember they are locals and well absorbed into the community. How welcoming is the community to outsiders? In some small towns, you might be greeted like long-lost family, or you might not be accepted until your family has lived there for at least seven generations! That can be lonely if you are used to a large social circle.

The affordability of property is important, but so is the overall cost of living and the job market if you plan to continue working. Consider the things you appreciate where you now live and compare that with your possible new home. The quality of medical care becomes vital as we age. Find out the availability and reputation of the local doctors, medical clinics, and hospitals. Also, learn about the services for seniors in your new community. Is there a Department or Office of Aging? What county or state programs are available? Many departments provide legal and insurance counseling and caregiver support, which are resources you may need in the future, if not immediately. Consider the shopping, restaurants, cultural activities, church groups, senior centers, gyms, festivals and events, and personal development, like auditing classes at the local college.

## BUYING YOUR OWN FARM

If you are lucky, you will find a place to live in a horse-friendly area. The property you want is zoned for agricultural use. Your biggest problems are practical ones about where to buy hay and how many horses you can convince your husband you need.

Even near major metropolitan centers, there are open acres a few miles outside of the congestion where you can have the best of both worlds—rural living, but close to urban amenities.

That happy situation might not last. More and more, developers gobble up farms and acreage and turn them into housing developments, condos, retail centers, and light industrial campuses. Ever-encroaching urban sprawl overtakes counties that were once known for their acres of rolling pastures and cultivated fields. Developers petition planning and zoning departments to change an area's designation from agricultural use to residential, commercial, or mixed-use, none of which accommodate horses. In many areas, horse owners don't know what's happening until they see big "For Sale" signs on properties or, worse, backhoes leveling trees and trucks hauling in construction equipment.

Seek out an experienced real estate agent who specializes in farm and equine properties and will know about the equestrian community (and availability of services, such as large animal vets and farriers) in the area. Planning and zoning regulations are often complex for farm acreage, especially when it is undeveloped. Property lines and easements sometimes require updated surveys and reviews of tax records to determine the exact dimensions of the property.

Your dream property may already have horses living on it. That should mean you are good to go for bringing in your own herd. You still must check to make sure of that. In some areas, there isn't any clear zoning about horses. It's possible that the owners never checked to see if there were zoning regulations, and no one ever complained. The farm might have been grandfathered when zoning in the area was changed, and that exception ends when the property changes hands. Your dream property could still be zoned agricultural, but the surrounding area is rezoned for some other use. You may find yourself in a situation where your farm can still be used for keeping horses, but you must pay taxes based on the new zoning for the surrounding area, and that is almost always a higher tax rate.

Assuming the zoning designation is favorable, you still must abide not only by zoning regulations but also planning department, health department, and sometimes engineering department requirements. Even if your property already has fencing and outbuildings, double-check that they meet the regulations. Often people didn't know approval was needed and either installed things without getting proper permission or installed things incorrectly. You don't want to add repairs, demolition, and reconstruction costs on top of a mortgage and your other anticipated expenses.

If the land has never been used for horse-keeping, work with your county extension office or a landscape architect as well as the planning and zoning offices to thoroughly assess the property. Plan your layout to minimize your workload.

Before you finish, you'll be an expert about wells and septic systems, setback distances for structures and fencing, run-off buffers to protect streams, and installing water pumps. Take advantage of the soil assessment through the county extension service to learn what you need to do to improve your pastures and where to place your manure pile.

Some people take "living with their horses" to a new level by designing a house/barn combination. The living quarters are above or adjacent to the stalls and the rest of the barn. It is the ultimate in convenience since you can literally step out of bed and into the feed room. While it is not a widespread trend, it has fans, particularly in areas with harsh winters. On the downside, you must consider equine aromas year-round and insects in the summer. Financing is sometimes tricky as lenders struggle to decide if the structure is a barn or a house, each with different mortgage and lending policies.

## OTHER HORSE-AT-HOME OPTIONS

If you want to live close to your horse but don't want to deal with all the complications of handling a farm, there are other options. Equine subdivisions and horse farm communities attract people who want a horse-oriented lifestyle that's easier to manage.

*Equine subdivisions*, also called *equine residential communities*, are neighborhoods of individual homes that share an equestrian center. These are almost always gated communities, which limit access to anyone except homeowners, and they are expensive. Even at those that advertise themselves as equine communities, fewer than half of the residents have horses or ride. The lots vary in size, generally between 1 and 5 acres. Depending on the development, horses are kept on the individual properties or at a common barn with shared paddocks and riding arenas. Many of the developments have trails or are near parks or public lands.

While some communities are relatively modest in amenities, high-end facilities may boast elegant barns and dedicated jump fields or indoor dressage arenas. There can be a resident horse trainer and/or riding instructor, and the facility hosts clinics. They often share a common veterinarian, farrier, dentist, and other professionals too, such as an equine bodyworker. Usually, hired staff handles feeding and barn chores.

In other communities, the owners perform those duties on a co-op basis. Many equine subdivisions also offer resort-style living, with horses being just one part of a mix that can include golf courses, spas, pools, fitness centers, restaurants, and clubhouses.

These developments work well for people who don't have as much time as they want to spend with their horses and can't or don't want to care for them personally. It's better than a boarding barn since the horses are very convenient. It's also nice to live in a horsey neighborhood where people don't drift away from you at parties when you start discussing your horse's refusal to load or how to treat an abscess.

A homeowner's association (HOA) dictates conditions with which property owners must comply. These include rules about the design and materials used for your house (many subdivisions specify the contractor and architect), landscaping, holiday decorations, noise, parking, trash, and recycling. Homeowners pay a fee that covers maintenance of common areas and other needs like maintaining private roads. In almost all instances, the equine facilities are a separate and additional fee. Be sure you fully understand the limitations, amenities, costs, conditions, and homeowner responsibilities before you buy.

*Horse farm communities* are gated communities containing individual farms of between 1 and 20 acres. Some communities have amenities like a community center with a clubhouse and swimming pool or a network of riding trails. Like the equine subdivisions, these communities are very costly. These are also governed by an HOA.

In many ways, it's the best of both worlds. You have your own farm and can care for your horses your way but still live near horse friends. This gives you a pool of support, advice, and help, which provides you with more freedom to travel, for instance, and assistance in emergencies.

*Shared community living* is a new idea and nascent movement. A group of people buy land together and set up "horse-keeping." They may live in the same house or have their own house or apartment, either on the property or somewhere nearby. Members of the community share the mortgage, construction and maintenance costs, feed, taxes, utilities, and other expenses. This is an extension of co-op barns where members share daily tasks. People considering joining a shared community must consider the long-term possibilities, like a member's illness or death, financial difficulties, lifestyle changes, or personality clashes.

# CHAPTER 19

# Boarders: Benefit or Bother?

To help cover costs and have a riding companion, you might consider taking in a boarder or two. If that's the case, you have a whole new set of considerations. The first of these is whether that's allowed by local zoning and planning regulations. Accepting boarders may affect your legal status. In many places, charging for the service makes you a business with legal, tax, and insurance ramifications. You must report your fees as income, which may affect your Social Security payment. If you live in an equine community, find out if the covenants allow you to have boarders.

## TYPES OF BOARD

The monthly boarding fee generally includes the cost of feed and hay and compensation for your time and energy. It should also consider additional services and expenses, like the cost of dewormers, holding the horse for vet or farrier, administering medications, additional feedings if required or requested, supplements, or special feed. As the stable owner, you have responsibilities for the health of the horses on your property. Before accepting a boarder, make sure the horse is up-to-date on all vaccinations and has a current negative Coggins test. In the boarding contract, include the requirement that the horse be on a vaccination schedule. It's a smart idea to review his medical records so you are aware of any past problems or conditions that could reappear. You can also include permission to contact your veterinarian in the case of an emergency should the horse's owner be unable to be reached.

You should charge enough to cover a portion of the insurance and develop a reserve for maintenance and repairs. Transportation to shows or clinics is usually calculated for the individual event.

You might also consider offering "field/pasture/self-care" board, as we discussed on p. 133. This means a horse owner pays a boarding fee to keep her horse at your stable but does much of the work herself. The fee for this arrangement is considerably less than full board.

Some stables require boarders to pay the first month's board and a security deposit, which is often equal to a month's board. This is like a landlord charging the first month's rent and a security deposit. Do not let the horse onto your property until the check for the first month's payment has cleared the bank. If you needed to buy any special supplies for the horse, they must also be paid for in advance for the first month. After that, include it in the board bill. This is just as true for a friend as it is for a stranger. Where money is concerned, boarding is a business, not a favor.

## CONTRACTS

You must have a written boarding contract. Never allow anyone to keep their horse on your property without a detailed, written contract. Handshake deals and doing favors for friends can quickly turn as sour as vinegar. Horse people are notoriously soft touches, and we are often taken advantage of because we don't want to seem mean and prefer to avoid conflicts.

An equine lawyer will draw up a thorough contract. Another option is to ask other stables to show you their paperwork. You can also find many sample contracts online. Most of those are fine for generalities but think about including things that might not be covered. The more details you include, the fewer problems you will have down the road.

Draw up a set of barn rules like we discussed on p. 42, and post them in the tack room or lounge. Include the rules in the boarding agreement. It gives you some authority to act and, if necessary, ask someone to leave if the rules are chronically ignored. A liability waiver should also be part of the contract. If the stable is in a state with an equine liability law, also known as an "inherent risk" law, include a copy of that in the contract and have the boarder initial it. This gives you a smidgen of protection in case of an accident, but liability insurance is still a must.

Spell out the procedure for non-payment, late payment, and abandonment. The late fee is usually an additional percent of the monthly bill, although some stables make it a flat additional daily fee. Sometimes seeing the actual number gets better results. Check out the local laws and spell out very clearly the consequences of non-payment, including seizing the horse.

To some extent, the boarder is responsible for damage done by her horse. This doesn't mean things like the occasional demolished water bucket or fence rail, although you can include them, but more considerable destruction to fencing, stalls, and equipment, which requires you to perform repairs or buy replacements and materials. While you should have a reserve to pay for some repairs beyond routine maintenance, it's fair to ask for at least partial reimbursement for serious damage. Note that in the boarding agreement, along with some indication of what constitutes "serious" damage.

Explain the plans for veterinarian visits, particularly vaccinations, and require that the boarder have the shots administered within the required vaccination period. The boarder pays the veterinarian directly. That protects you from an unpaid invoice. Have the same requirement for the farrier, saddle fitter, and dentist.

Specify how much notice you expect if the boarder wants to move. In general, it is 30 days, which gives you a chance to find another boarder without loss of income. If a boarder leaves early, the remainder of the month's board is usually pro-rated.

Include procedures for removing a disruptive or dangerous horse. The definitions are open to interpretation, but if you decide that an animal is putting you, other boarders, or anyone else at the stable in danger, you can insist that the horse goes. It can be as long as 30 days or as short as "tomorrow." Remember that you can be held responsible if the animal injures someone, even when waivers were signed.

Most places allow boarders to store their trailer on the property for no charge. However, whether you charge for storage or not, insist that they provide proof of insurance for theft or damage.

**Power of Attorney**

Require the boarder to give you a Power of Attorney, such as I explained on p. 154. This allows you to make medical and veterinary decisions concerning the horse's care and treatment, including euthanasia if the owner cannot be reached. Before you accept the horse, make sure you and the owner have discussed the decisions you might have to make in an emergency, including her wishes for the treatment of the horse and his quality of life, the expectation of recovery, and costs for treatment so that you both understand and are comfortable with the possibilities. Without that written permission, you could face legal problems if the owner disagrees with your actions.

You can also include procedures for evacuation and other steps to deal with emergencies. Specify what actions you would take to deal with natural disasters and weather events.

## Insurance

Insurance for yourself and your boarders is another major concern. Make sure you know in detail what your farm and homeowner's policies cover. Work with an insurance broker who specializes in equine and farm insurance to find the most appropriate policy. Protect yourself as thoroughly as possible. Insurance on equine property is often expensive, but lawyer fees run several hundred dollars an hour, and without proper coverage, you could lose your farm and your horses.

As I mentioned on p. 152, liability protection is vital. No matter what happens on your property, you can be held liable. In today's litigious society, you will probably be sued. Do not rely on "inherent risk" laws or "hold harmless" agreements for protection. Visitors should still sign a waiver, even if they've just stopped by to watch a friend ride or see a newborn foal. Accusations of negligence weaken those "hold harmless" protections. Insurance companies and lawyers work diligently to find ways to get a good settlement for their clients and recoup any damage payments.

In addition, your coverage can be affected when boarders do not carry their own liability insurance. Strongly encourage, if not require, that boarders get liability insurance. It is not expensive. In general, a few hundred dollars a year provides up to one million dollars of coverage. If they are reluctant, explain that it protects them. If their horse should injure someone or damage property, they can be paying medical bills or the cost of repairs.

Make very sure that your boarders understand that the insurance policy on your farm and property does not cover their tack, equipment, or possessions. They must provide that coverage themselves. That's something that boarders often don't realize until after a theft, fire, or natural disaster.

## FIRING A BOARDER

Boarders can be an asset to your barn. They bring in income; they provide companions for riding; they can help with chores; they help create the equine community you love.

But boarders can also be a source of frustration. They may be chronic late- or non-payers. Some boarders constantly complain, question your procedures, or display a sour attitude. That can quickly undermine the pleasant ambiance you want to develop. If your other boarders grow frustrated, they might move to another barn. That hurts your income as well as giving your place a poor reputation that discourages others from boarding with you.

If you have such a boarder, first try diplomacy. Have a private conversation. Ask about the problems she is having at the stable and the reasons for her complaints. It might be a situation of just needing to clear the air or explaining why the procedures and rules are what they are. If she is a new horse owner, she may not have experience or knowledge and could be reacting poorly to cover up her naivete. Often, the behavior results from stress or issues that have nothing to do with the stable. When there are financial problems, try to work something out if you want to do so. Beware, however, that chronic late payers have heartbreaking stories about the difficulties in their personal lives that are causing their financial woes, which usually means they are not planning to pay you. They know that you will not refuse to feed their horse and will string you along for as long as they can. The reality is that business is business. When a boarder has personal issues, that is unfortunate, but you don't own that situation. Your first responsibility is to your operation and the other people at your stable.

If the situation does not improve or you do not want to deal with the drama, you can ask the boarder to leave. Point out that she does not seem happy or satisfied and that since it is not working out, she'd be happier elsewhere. You can either choose to deal with her attitude or behavior for the full 30 days or offer to pro-rate the board if she leaves sooner. However, insist that she be gone in 30 days or run the risk of the drama continuing indefinitely.

There is no point in getting into an argument, although that's sometimes very tempting. You must be professional. Do not discuss the situation with anyone at the stable or within your circle of friends. If you do, it will undoubtedly be passed around and take on a life of its own with embellishments that probably have no relation to the actual situation. If you have other boarders, they will know the story and can defend you. Likewise, under no circumstances should you take to social media in any form to publicize the situation, even if she complains about you. If you respond, you simply breathe life into the drama and keep it going.

CHAPTER 20

# Barn Fires, Natural Disasters, and Evacuations

T here are many brochures and documents that provide essential information and advice in preparing for and dealing with the topics covered in this section. Links to them are found in Resources and at www.ridersofacertainage.com.

## BARN FIRES

Few things create such an immediate, nauseating, stomach-churning dread as the thought of a barn fire. The thought of our horses being trapped in an inferno is terrifying. Those who suffer such a disaster never completely recover from it.

Barns are tinderboxes of dry wood, hay, straw, bedding, blankets, cobwebs (yes, cobwebs burn), fast food wrappers, towels, leg wraps, and dozens of other flammable materials. Sometimes gasoline, oil, fertilizer, and other accelerants are stashed in storage areas. Tractors, other motorized equipment, and gas-powered leaf blowers are parked in the breezeway. The electrical system is often a tangle of residential-grade extension cords running from an aged panel box.

It takes very little to ignite a barn fire, and it spreads with stunning speed. Fire reaching a stall will consume the bedding in two to three minutes. A horse in that stall must get out within 30 seconds or be overcome by carbon monoxide and heat. After 30 seconds, an uncontrolled barn fire can be so intense that a hand-held fire extinguisher will not contain it. A barn will be fully involved in 7 to 10 minutes and usually burns to the ground within 20.

Invite your local fire department to inspect your barn and property. They will evaluate everything from their perspective. This also helps them to pinpoint your location. Often GPS and street addresses are not entirely accurate, particularly in more remote areas.

The leading causes of barn fires are careless electrical malfunctions or misuse, smoking, spontaneous combustion of hay, and lightning strikes. With the exception of lightning, the danger can be reduced if not eliminated.

## Electrical Fires

Electrical faults and heating devices cause 50 percent of barn fires. Particularly in older buildings, the wiring and electrical outlets are often worn, overloaded, and not up to code. Conduit boxes are corroded, mice nibble wiring, plugs are loose, extension cords loop around supports, and dust covers the outlets. The circuit breaker box is often working beyond its limits, and none of the circuits is marked. Frequently, there are warning signs that a fire is imminent, like the smell of something melting, outlets or appliances that are hot to the touch, or flickering lights.

Faulty electrical appliances are responsible for many fires. Most often, the source is a box fan used to cool the stalls in the summer. Most people use residential box fans, which often run 24/7. They are not intended for that kind of continuous use. It strains and overheats the motor. Since the motors are inevitably covered with dust, it's even more likely that they will overheat. To safely cool your stalls, look for commercial and industrial fans. Many of these can be mounted over the stalls.

Winter brings another set of dangers in the form of heaters. Under no circumstances should any type of heater be left unattended. Space heaters, heat lamps, and dairy barn heaters are responsible for most winter fires. Usually, the heaters are placed too close to something flammable. "Coil" heaters are particularly hazardous because the coils are so hot that anything that touches them ignites instantly. Safer options are "radiator" and "ceramic" heaters. They have automatic cut-offs when they tip over or overheat. Immersible heaters for water buckets grow incredibly hot. If you are distracted by other chores and forget about the heater, it can boil away the water and continue to generate heat, possibly igniting things around it.

Have a licensed electrician inspect your barn and outbuildings. Place the electrical panel/circuit breaker box in an easily reachable spot and clearly label every circuit. Use light bulb safety cages on all exposed lights in the barn and know the proper wattage for each fixture. Outlets should have a dust shield/weather shield cover. Have a master power cutoff switch on the outside of the barn. Mount handheld ABC fire extinguishers at each entrance to the barn. ABC extinguishers are designed for electrical fires. Check them annually to make sure they are charged. Never use water to try to put out an electrical fire. Water conducts electricity, and you will get shocked or electrocuted.

## Smoking

Fortunately, fires caused by smoking are the easiest to avoid. Simply prohibit smoking on the property. Ban cigarettes, pipes, cigars, joints, and "e-cigarettes" (although the incidents are rare, e-cigarettes have been known to explode and ignite flammable materials). The ban includes inside and outside the barn, outbuildings, fields or paddocks, and parking areas. A stray ember from a tossed cigarette can ignite trash, debris, brush, and weeds. As a general precaution, clear all of that away from the barn area. Stray bits of hay touching heat sources such as exhaust tailpipes or motors of a tractor or other equipment ignite easily. Store

## *In the Case of a Fire*

If there is a fire:

➤ Call the fire department.

➤ Turn off the master electrical switch.

➤ Use the cut-off valve for any propane tank, natural gas, or LP lines.

➤ If possible, evacuate the horses. Take them to a secure holding area. If they are loose, they may run back into the barn or gallop into the road.

➤ Open any access gates to the property and keep the roads clear for fire vehicles. The driveways and other access should be wide enough for trucks and equipment, which is something you need to address before an emergency.

➤ Make sure any hydrants or pumps are working and accessible.

➤ After the fire, have your vet check all the horses, particularly for signs of smoke inhalation. Also, check to ensure that no embers landed under their hair. When this happens, the horses can suffer burns that smolder along their skin, sometimes for days, before anyone notices the injury.

gasoline, oil, paint, and other flammables away from the barn. Keep trash cans covered and empty them regularly.

### Spontaneous Combustion

There is a great feeling of satisfaction and security in seeing a hayloft filled with neatly stacked bales of hay. There is also a danger because hay can ignite under the right conditions without ever coming near an open flame.

It's called "spontaneous combustion." It happens when the temperature inside a bale of hay becomes hot enough to burn. This occurs with hay that was not fully dry before it was baled. If the bales are stacked so tightly that air cannot circulate around them, the risk rises. Hay catches fire within one to five minutes of reaching ignitable temperatures. The rest of the haystack almost immediately ignites.

Usually, the fire starts about six weeks after the hay is baled. There are several warning signs. You might see steam rising from the bales. There may be condensation on the roof or eaves of the barn, or you may notice mold on those surfaces. You may smell a hot, caramel-like, musty, acrid, or tobacco-like aroma.

When this happens, immediately contact the fire department and follow its instructions. Evacuate the barn and move equipment away from the area.

### Lightning Strikes

Lightning is the one fire threat that cannot be prevented. Nine out of 10 barns struck by lightning are totaled, usually burning to the ground within minutes. This is not surprising because a lightning bolt is five times hotter than the sun. While lightning rods do not reduce the odds of your barn being struck, they do minimize the damage by directing the energy into the ground.

Lightning is attracted to metal objects, like power lines, metal roofs, automatic waterers, and pump handles. It also strikes tall and isolated objects like a run-in shed or a solitary tree in a field. It is not attracted to water, but the electricity travels through damp ground. This is why horses standing in a field are killed even though the lightning bolt did not actually hit them.

Lightning can strike as far as 10 miles from the storm that generates it. To keep yourself safe, take cover as soon as you hear thunder and stay inside until 30 minutes after you hear the last rumble. If your barn is grounded, bring your horses inside. If not, try to keep them away from wire fences, water pumps, and other likely targets.

### Sprinkler Systems

A sprinkler system can put out a fire or at least slow its progress. Sprinkler systems are expensive and require a reliable water source. Smoke, heat, and flame detectors are equipped with alarms and are often connected to the fire department. They do not put out the fire but alert you and possibly buy time to address it.

While both lightning rods and sprinkler systems are expensive to install, many insurance companies offer huge discounts to farms that have them because barn fires are one of their most frequent claims.

## Natural Disasters

Mother Nature gives us perfect spring days with blooming crocuses and humming-birds, beautiful summer scenery to enjoy on a trail ride, autumn days painted with glowing leaves, and rides through the snow on crisp, cold mornings. That's when she is in a good mood. When she hasn't had her coffee, she can turn vicious and hit us with hurricanes, wildfires, tornadoes, and blizzards. While we can't prevent natural disasters, we can do a lot to prepare for Mother Nature's tantrums and minimize their impact. (There are several excellent, detailed handbooks and guides for dealing with natural disasters published by agencies and experts in disaster planning. Links to them are at www.ridersofacertainage.com.)

While each disaster has unique characteristics, many of the steps for preparation and action are the same for any weather event. Start with your property. Know what is covered by your insurance policies. Some policies consider storm damage to be an "Act of God" and, therefore, uninsurable. Others cover only certain types of damage or put limits on how much they will pay. Almost all policies require proof of damage as part of the claims process. For that reason, taking photos of your property before the disaster is vital.

Just as you should do for general insurance purposes (see p. 153), take time-stamped photos of everything: land and landscaping; trees and where they are in relation to buildings; barns and outbuildings (both interior and exterior); tractors, manure spreaders, golf carts; everything in your tack room; hay storage area; and feed room. Include your grooming kit, buckets, saddle pads, blankets, even down to bottles of fly spray. You will be stunned at how much stuff you have. General photos of a room or area are acceptable, but big-ticket items should be photographed individually. In the case of saddles and other equipment with serial numbers, make sure you show them. Upload the photos onto a storage system where they can be easily sent to the claims adjuster. In addition, copies of those photos should be with the deeds, vehicle titles, wills, passports, birth certificates, and high-value items like jewelry in a safe deposit box.

Claims adjusters are delighted when they have a physical inventory and solid numbers to work with instead of forcing a client to try to recall everything from memory. The more documentation they have, the easier it is for them to process your claim quickly and the better the chance you have of getting a reasonable settlement.

Invest in a generator. Learn how to hook it up and practice until it becomes second nature. Fill several jerry cans with additional gas but do not store them in a shed or the barn. Do not operate a generator in an enclosed area like a garage or barn. They emit dangerous fumes.

If you don't already know your neighbors, now is the time to get acquainted. Develop a group disaster plan. Create a telephone tree so that you can reach each other quickly. Discuss sharing trailer space to move horses and sharing hay and feed in the event of an evacuation.

## Evacuations

Sometimes a natural disaster requires evacuating horses to a safer location. Planning and preparation are key to handling this successfully. The PETS Act that was passed in the aftermath of Hurricane Katrina requires FEMA (Federal Emergency Response Agency) to include pets in their emergency planning and management. However, livestock and large animals are exempt from the law. Some localities may include livestock in their operations, but, in general, horse owners are on their own.

The single most important preparation for evacuation is this: teach your horse to load into the trailer. Particularly in the case of wildfires, you do not have time to deal with a stubborn horse.

Work with a trainer if you are struggling to teach your horse to load. Online videos from many trainers demonstrate effective trailer loading. Hook up the trailer and practice once or twice a month. If possible, teach your horse to load in as many different types of trailer as possible. In an emergency, you might not have a choice of transportation. Teach your horse to be led with just a rope around its neck, by its ear, and while wearing a blindfold. If your trailer backing skills are less than accomplished, connect with someone who is good at it and can teach you how to master that critical ability.

Knowing where to go is the overriding question about evacuation. The National Equine Emergency Evacuation Directory is a free online resource. It connects people needing to evacuate with a network of volunteers offering stabling, transportation, search and rescue, and other services, like veterinarians and farriers. It is organized and operated by Fleet of Angels. This national non-profit organization provides assistance to horse owners in emergencies. They coordinate with FEMA and national agencies, state emergency offices, and other groups during a crisis to provide accurate information, advice, and effective services.

## Hurricanes

Of all the natural disasters that horse owners face, hurricanes are probably the easiest to prepare for. Hurricane season officially runs from June through November but named storms have appeared as early as April and have rolled across the Caribbean as late as December.

It takes as long as two weeks from the time a tropical wave develops off the coast of Africa until it becomes a full-blown (and blowing) hurricane churning toward Florida, the Gulf of Mexico, or the Atlantic Seaboard. During that time,

# Evacuation Checklist

### For Your Horse

➤ Pack up-to-date medical and shot records and Coggins tests. Include a health certificate if you travel to another state. While some states waive the requirement for a health certificate during an emergency, you can't count on that courtesy. Have necessary medications prepared and ready to be grabbed at the last moment.

➤ Put identification on your horse. He can get separated at evacuation centers or on the road if someone else is moving him. Write your name and contact number on the horse in livestock crayon or use a broodmare collar. Some people make dog tags and weave them into the horse's mane.

➤ Pack enough hay and grain for one week and water for two days.

➤ Bring halters, lead ropes, buckets, fly sheets, hoses.

### For Your Pets

➤ Pack food for a week, blankets and extra leashes or carriers.

➤ Bring proof of rabies and other vaccinations.

➤ Check with your vet for tranquilizers if any of your pets are prone to nerves in unfamiliar situations.

➤ It's a smart idea to have a muzzle for dogs. Even the most mellow Labrador can bite in fear. In a pinch, use Vetrap or rolled gauze.

### For Yourself

➤ Pack your trailer with everything you might need for your horse and pets as soon as evacuation appears possible.

➤ Pack and load for yourself in advance. Bring enough clothing, medicines, and toiletries for a week.

## AGELESS ADVICE

➤ Pack any medications you are taking and know how to refill prescriptions. After some disasters, people are homeless or in transient living situations for weeks. Getting refills can be difficult.

➤ If you have a serious medical condition, bring copies of your medical records. There's no guarantee of providers being able to contact your physician or of your physician having access to her office or records.

➤ Bring knee, ankle, and wrist supports if you've ever used them and might have a flare-up of the condition.

➤ Gas up your tow vehicle and hitch up your trailer.

➤ Have at least one phone charger, a battery/solar powered/crank powered/ USB connection weather radio, extra batteries, flashlights, and a multi-purpose tool like a Leatherman.

➤ Carry several days' worth of non-perishable or freeze-dried food (you can almost always find hot water).

➤ Withdraw several hundred dollars of cash from your bank account. Credit cards can't be used when power is out, and if you evacuate, many places demand cash from out-of-towners.

➤ Buy a CB radio. Weather can take down cell towers, and the systems can easily be overloaded, so don't rely on cell phones for communication. CBs allow for immediate updates and advice on local situations. State police and many local police and emergency agencies monitor CB channels.

forecasters predict storm tracks, the intensity of the winds, and possible storm surges. Disaster preparedness teams ready shelters, issue advisories, and position supplies. For horse people, decades of dealing with the storms gives us a lot of strategies for surviving the big blow as safely as possible.

Every state with a history of dealing with hurricanes publishes detailed advice online and through agriculture and extension services. Markel Insurance, a major insurer of horses and farms, has a concise brochure with advice on preparing for hurricanes and dealing with their aftermath. (A link to the brochure is at www. ridersofacertainage.com.)

If there is any chance of your barn being flooded or hit by a storm surge, you must evacuate. Don't assume that because you are not on the water that you are safe. The storm surge from Hurricane Katrina swept eight miles inland from Lake Pontchartrain. South of New Orleans, horses trapped in stalls at farms considered on high ground drowned. If you cannot move the horses, leave them loose. The wild horses on the barrier islands of Maryland, North Carolina, and Virginia have survived storms for three hundred years.

Evacuate no later than 72 hours before predicted landfall. The most practical reason is that waiting any longer puts you in the middle of traffic jams, hunting for gas or diesel, and trying to reach shelters that are already full. As the winds pick up, the dangers of hauling a trailer increase. Winds over 40 mph trigger dangerous driving conditions for any high-sided vehicle like a trailer.

### Wildfires

The past few years have been nightmares for the western United States as wildfires charred thousands of acres of land and killed hundreds of people. Climatologists and meteorologists predict more prolonged and more intense fire seasons.

There is little you can do to prevent a wildfire, but you can take steps to limit its impact. Clear vegetation at least 30 feet from any building. Keep the area mowed. Consider adding a goat or two to your menagerie. They thrive on grazing dry brush. But appreciate that nothing can withstand the fury of a raging wildfire.

Plan for fire season by assuming that you will need to evacuate at some point and that you won't have much time to move when the order comes. If you cannot evacuate your horses, turn them out in pastures or paddocks. Use rope halters with "breakaway" strips. Do not use nylon or leather halters. The nylon will melt in high heat, and the metal buckles and cheek pieces become hot and cause burns. Open the gates but close the barn doors and block any route that leads back to the barn.

The atmosphere near a fire can damage your horse's lungs. He is breathing in the same smoke that has you wearing a bandana or mask. It's filled with carbon dioxide and carbon monoxide, plus soot and particulates from melting plastics, household materials, wood, chemicals, tires, and other contaminants. Horses' lungs are huge, and these tiny particles get deep into them, affecting their respiration and causing airway obstructions and lung damage.

If you evacuate, monitor your horse's respiration when you arrive at the evacuation center. Signs of respiratory distress include cough, nasal discharge, wheezing, a heart rate over 30 beats per minute, flaring nostrils, and struggling to breathe. Lung damage can cause pneumonia, which can take a week or more to develop. Check your horse's coat and mane for burns. Cinders get underneath the coat, causing burns that aren't always immediately noticed. The University of California at Davis provides advice on monitoring your horse and what to do if you see signs of trouble. (Find a link at www.ridersofacertainage.com.)

If you must leave your horse behind, contact a veterinarian as soon as possible when you return to your barn to assess his condition. Assume there is lung damage. When there are burns, take photos and send them to the vet so she can assess the horse's condition. Follow her instructions regarding treatment. When she says it is okay, provide free-choice water and hay. These help to keep the horse calm and maintain gut function.

## Tornadoes

When storm clouds gather in the South and Midwest, people monitor their local radio and TV channels and pay close attention to The Weather Channel. It's tornado season, and powerful, destructive storms are lurking in the skies. While hurricanes give you time to prepare, tornadoes appear with little warning.

The National Weather Service (NWS) issues two levels of alerts. A tornado Watch means that conditions are ripe for tornadoes to develop. A tornado Warning means that a funnel cloud has been spotted on the ground or that radar has detected circulation in the clouds. In either case, if you are in the area, you must take cover immediately.

There is also a TORCON rating. This is not official information from the NWS. Created and used by The Weather Channel, it is a scale of 1 to 10, which estimates a tornado's chances within 50 miles of a location that day. The higher the number, the more chance of a tornado forming. It does not estimate the size or severity of the tornado.

Whether to bring the horses into the barn or leave them outside in Watches and Warnings is a bigger gamble than picking the Trifecta at Churchill Downs on Derby Day. Tornadoes are notoriously capricious. The roof of a concrete barn can collapse onto the stalls beneath, or the winds can carry it away without moving a single bale of hay in the hayloft. Horses left outside because there was no time to bring them in are unharmed while the barn where they would have taken shelter disintegrates.

There are a few things you can do to prepare. Store anything that could become a projectile in the most secure room in the barn. Put fly masks on horses to minimize the chances of eye injuries from flying debris. Blankets or rain sheets provide more body protection. Use only breakaway halters so that horses won't get caught in debris.

When you are under a Warning, turn off the power and natural gas lines. Go into the sturdiest place in the barn. Put on a riding helmet. Emergency rooms report that many victims of tornadoes have head injuries caused by flying debris or from being trapped under collapsing structures. If you have a safety vest, wear it as another layer of protection. Cover yourself with a horse blanket.

After the storm passes, tend to any injuries to yourself and your companions first. You can't help the horses when you are incapacitated. Use your phone to call for help but expect service to be limited. Texting is sometimes more effective. Check for downed power lines. Check the horses for injuries. Be alert that they will probably be traumatized and reactive. Collect the horses into one area. If possible, provide clean water and hay, but do not use anything that might be contaminated with chemicals or pesticides. If any animals are dead, notify authorities to arrange for removal.

### Blizzards and Ice Storms

A vista of freshly fallen snow may be the stuff of Hallmark cards, but Mother Nature's winter mantle brings a lot of challenges for horsewomen. Start preparing for winter long before the temperatures begin to drop. Thanks to climate change, Southerners can no longer rely on sub-freezing temperatures and blizzards staying up north. And in the rest of the country, you can no longer depend on that first cold snap not happening until October.

The best preparation is up-to-date maintenance. Inspect your barn and outbuildings for holes, cracks, missing shingles, loose siding, and rotting wood. Inspect the gutters and install snow guards. Align the barn doors so that they move freely in their tracks and latch securely. Lay down footing material in mud-prone and heavy traffic areas. Have a place to dump manure from the barn if your usual spot is unreachable.

As mentioned earlier, only use space heaters with extreme caution as they are a fire hazard.

During snowstorms, horses are usually okay when they can reach a run-in shed or windbreak, even in heavy snow. However, a blizzard, deep snow, extreme cold, high winds, freezing rain, or ice require you to protect the horses. You may have to get creative if you do not have enough stalls by using cross-ties, panels from the round pen, and strategically parked tractors, wheelbarrows, manure spreaders, or golf carts to create spaces in the barn or on the most protected side of an outbuild-ing. On ice, spread shavings, sand, or bedding to create safer footing.

If you decide to stay in the barn, provide for your comfort. Stock up on hand and foot warmers. Buy a stocking cap with a LED light for hands-free lighting while working in the dark. Have a sleeping bag, dry clothing, battery or crank-powered cell phone charger, and a lamp and extra batteries. If you have a microwave, great. But do not be tempted to use a camp propane stove in the barn to heat food. Rely on non-perishable food. Remember that ice cream keeps just fine in snow.

# CHAPTER 21

# On the Road:
# Money, Medicine, and Practicalities

The RV lifestyle appeals to many seniors. Traveling around the country in your recreational vehicle, visiting National Parks, touring historic sites, spending winters in Arizona and summers in Maine. Trick out an RV just the way you want it, join the Good Sam Club, and hit the road. It's a great reward after decades of obligations and stress.

Horse owners want to do the same thing, but naturally they want to make the journey with their horses. Online groups and magazines dedicated to the "happy trails" lifestyle post dozens of "between the ears" pictures and shots of landscapes taken at picturesque destinations. Posts tell of great adventures at exciting destinations. Riders forge new friendships and create lifelong memories. You're eager to buy a trailer with living quarters, load the horses, and wave goodbye to your neighbors as you drive off into the sunset.

It can be a great life, and for many people, it is. As with any other significant life change, it's wise to recognize the reality versus the dream before committing yourself. There are online websites and social media groups dedicated to equine trailer life.

Some are regional, while others are clearinghouses for information about good trails and campgrounds across the country. Specialized sites offer advice on maintenance and life hacks. Those are all good groups to follow to get a realistic idea of what living with your horse involves. (A current list is at www.ridersofacertainage.com.)

Women traveling alone, particularly older women, are vulnerable, be it from physical threats on the trail or at campsites, or from opportunistic repair shops, service providers, or campsite operators. The nomadic equine lifestyle is best if you travel with or regularly meet up with a group. The solo lifestyle can become lonely, and if you have problems—a breakdown or sudden medical issue—dealing with them alone adds to the difficulty.

As always, preparing for the unexpected is the best way to guarantee that your plans are not derailed. Work with a local mechanic to learn the basics of your engine and mechanical terminology. Just knowing the vocabulary gives you a layer of protection from repair shops that consider women easy marks for unneeded work and jacked-up prices. Learn how to change a tire on both your truck and trailer. Carry tools for simple repairs and know how to use them. Don't trust that any male knows more about mechanics than you do. They are often just as uneducated and just as prone to being taken advantage of. The National RV Training Academy offers an "Educated RV Owners" home study course for basic maintenance and repair, which is suitable for trailers with living quarters. It also offers a week-long, in-person class at its headquarters in Texas.

For security on horseback, find a "self-defense on the trail" clinic or study online videos. Practice the techniques with friends. Some people arm themselves on the trail. The professionals who teach these courses say that realistically the odds of you reaching your handgun and using it effectively while you are fighting panic, your horse is dancing around, and someone is trying to pull you off your saddle are very slim. If you want to "fire" something at an attacker, an option is to carry wasp spray in a shoulder sleeve. It is legal everywhere. It shoots a directed spray up to 20 feet with a finger squeeze and incapacitates the attacker. Try this while mounted first to sensitize your horse to the noise and for you to practice the technique. Other people carry a loud whistle that can startle and scare off an attacker. (You will need to desensitize your horse to this.)

## MEDICAL, FINANCIAL, AND LICENSING ISSUES

The dull, practical matters get in the way of the fun of dreaming about your new life. The immediate ones are financial. Most full-time horse campers say it's no more expensive than living at home, but everyone's situation is different.

One significant factor for us is the availability and quality of health care. Medical insurance is a major concern. Several companies specialize in health insurance plans for those living on the road and are worth investigating. If you have Medicare, that's a good start. But you must still consider Medicare supplemental, dental and vision, and long-term care coverages. Some of these plans are valid only in limited geographic areas or require treatment from a network of doctors and hospitals that may not include your destinations. Private insurance for those not yet on Medicare is expensive and often has similar limitations. Short-

### AGELESS ADVICE

## *Nomad Needs*

Many companies provide insurance advice and policies for "nomads." Other firms coordinate medical assistance. Examples of their products and services are mentioned in the following pages. The most current list and links to those companies and agencies are found at www.ridersofacertainage.com. Inclusion on this list does not imply a recommendation.

term medical plans that provide coverage for several weeks to several months are a potential solution if your regular plan won't work. However, many of them do not cover pre-existing conditions.

If you need routine medical tests, you can order many of them online or over the phone without needing a physician's order. Several nationwide lab companies allow you to schedule bloodwork and some other tests at a local facility. Payment is via credit card, and your results are back within two days. If you have prescriptions, check with your physician to see about prescription options. Some insurance programs network with national drug store chains so that you can refill prescriptions anywhere in the country.

Even the most thorough insurance coverage means nothing if you can't find a doctor. Fortunately, there are many options. For immediate, non-critical situations, walk-in medical clinics are widely available and provide good care for minor complaints and injuries, some tests, and referrals for more treatment. Most of them will bill insurance companies, although not all; you may still get a bill. The Remote Area Medical Volunteer Corps (RAM) holds free clinics in rural areas that provide medical, dental, and vision screenings and treatment. The schedule and location of clinics are on its website.

There's a long waiting list for doctor's appointments in many towns, and a good number of physicians will not see patients who do not live in the area. Veterans using the VA system face the same problem of long wait times for appointments. Fortunately, technology comes to the rescue. Telemedicine means that you can connect with a physician by internet wherever you are for a consultation, referral to a specialist, or obtaining a prescription. "Doctor visits" can be visual using your computer or smart phone's camera, through Zoom, Skype, or similar conferencing programs, by telephone, online chat, even via email. Some companies allow you to choose a doctor who becomes your primary care physician. This is a particularly attractive option when you have a complex medical history. If you need treatment on the road by doctors or facilities who don't know your history, their ability to consult your physician provides a level of understanding of your condition and better continuity of care.

It is vital that you keep copies of your medical records with you. These include Living Wills and Advance Directives. Record them on a thumb drive and print them out so that you can give them to physicians or hospitals. Also, upload them to the cloud for access under any circumstances. Some papers and legal documents, like deeds to property, should stay in a safe deposit box back home. The originals of Advance Directives and Living Wills should also be stored there. Authorize someone to access the box if you cannot do so.

With a bit of planning, dealing with your finances is straightforward and uncomplicated. Thanks to online banking, it's easy to access your bank accounts. Direct deposit takes care of getting pension and Social Security checks. Set up as many direct debit and electronic payments as you can. Use mobile banking to pay bills and transfer money between accounts. Many merchants accept cashless payments using your bank accounts through your smartphone and credit cards.

Notify your credit card companies that you will be traveling extensively and give them some idea of where you may be. If you expect to have any unusually large charges, let them know this in advance, too. It can spare you the headache of having a charge questioned or declined because of possible fraud. Consider getting a credit card to be used exclusively for sudden, unexpected major expenses, like vet bills or major truck or trailer repairs. This avoids the possibility of hitting the limit on your other cards.

Some states impose residency and driver's license requirements and vehicle registration for "snowbirds," those people who live in the state for several months each year but primarily reside elsewhere. In some cases, your trailer is then considered a second home with tax implications. Online groups for permanent nomads are good sources for the latest updates. You can also check with your auto insurance company and roadside travel companies like AAA. State DMV (Department of Motor Vehicle) websites are the place to look for license and registration information, although the sites are frequently hard to navigate. In addition, some states require you to have a Commercial Driver's License (CDL) for certain-sized rigs, usually those motorhomes that are the size of buses. That information is also on the DMV sites.

More and more, access to internet services is vital. From locating layovers and repair facilities, accessing online banking, and checking your email, to streaming entertainment, getting online is no longer optional. Many locations, however, don't have reliable Wi-Fi. Several companies provide the equipment and technology for remote access almost anywhere. If you are not sure where you will be—particularly if you want to go far off the beaten path—it's a good investment.

### Making Traveling Easier for Your Horse

Now that you've taken care of the practicalities for your travel, it's time to turn to your horse. You may be used to trailering him to local shows, trail rides, and perhaps even the occasional weekend camping trip. But long-distance travel and extended periods on the road require additional planning.

First on the list is a thorough medical checkup. This doesn't have to be as involved as a pre-purchase exam, but it should be more than a review of vital signs and up-to-date vaccinations. Talk your plans over with your veterinarian. Let her know the kind of riding and living conditions you expect. Listen to her advice, particularly if your horse has a history of lameness or colic. Depending on your horse's age and medical history, there may be other tests and checks she'll want to make. She may also recommend additional vaccinations based on where you are traveling to protect against regional diseases that may not appear in your area. Most often, those should be administered a month before you take to the road.

You will need a health certificate and a negative Coggins test if you are traveling out-of-state. The certificate confirms that your horse was healthy and showing no signs of any illness when he was examined. Depending on your state and your destination, the certificate is good for 30 to 90 days. Some states require that you stop at an agriculture checkpoint at the border and present the certificate. Failure to do so can result in a hefty fine. In addition, some states require that you present a health certificate when you leave the state. Each state's requirements are on their Agriculture Department's website.

If the certificate expires while you are traveling, you must arrange for an examination by a veterinarian. As mentioned elsewhere, you should carry a Power of Attorney and checklist of important contacts in an easy-to-identify folder in the cab of your tow vehicle.

A logical concern is finding a veterinarian in an unfamiliar location. Most campgrounds, as well as feedstores and tack shops, will know the local veterinarians. The American Association of Equine Practitioners has a "Get-A-DVM" directory on its website (www.aaep.org). You should also invest in a quality, comprehensive first aid kit and learn how to use it. Ask your veterinarian or experienced barn manager or horse trainer to teach you basic equine first aid. There are several excellent books about horse care and treating equine health emergencies you can carry with you (see www.ridersofacertainage.com). Read up on the most common injuries and illnesses so you can recognize them and have a rough plan for treatment.

Trailering is always stressful to your horse. Even if it's something as simple as an hour's trip to a trail ride or show, you can count on him showing the most common indication of nerves—a pile of poop in the trailer. By the time you start your trip, you should be familiar with your horse's idiosyncrasies when he travels. Some horses will refuse to eat or drink or will be very tense. Others trot onto the trailer and eagerly watch the landscape roll by. If your horse is the nervous type, ask your veterinarian about starting to feed a calming supplement before your travel or administering a mild relaxing drug.

On the trip, make sure your horse has constant access to hay. While some might not even sniff it, others "graze" throughout the trip. Equally important is that the horse have water. Offer water at every stop. Many horses will not drink, however. Unless he shows signs of dehydration, this is generally not a concern. However, if he refuses water when you arrive at your destination, monitor him for signs of dehydration and colic. Consider adding electrolytes to the water to encourage the horse to drink. Some horses will drink "molasses water": add molasses to your water until it has the appearance of gingerbread batter (this amount will vary depending on the size of the container you are using). Most horses love the flavor. Molasses water is also useful if your horse does not like the taste of water at your destination. When you use molasses water, make sure there is also regular water available. Place the buckets side-by-side.

Always carry one to two days of extra feed, hay, and water in case a breakdown, weather event, or other crisis disrupts your plans.

Whatever kind of traveler he is, you should work to make him comfortable. Most people install rubber floor mats to provide cushioning. Minimize dust in the trailer. Dust-free shavings help absorb urine and eliminate ammonia. Many people find this also provides better footing and cushioning. In stock trailers, however, shavings can fly around, which can cause respiratory troubles. They can also get into your horse's eyes. Using a fly mask eliminates that concern.

Some common matters of debate include:

*Box stall versus standing stall.* Many veterinarians and shippers prefer an open box stall in a trailer. The argument is that this allows the horse more freedom of movement, so that he is better able to balance himself. Others say that a standing stall allows the horse to brace himself in stop-and-go situations and to (God forbid) be more secure in an accident.

*To tie or not to tie.* If you tie your horse's head, make sure there is enough slack for him to easily lower his head and move it comfortably. Be careful what kind of knot you use. Many people create a daisy-chain of interconnecting loops. It's a form of quick-release, similar to the string tapes on bags of feed. However, if pulled in the wrong sequence, the rope knots. In normal circumstances, that's annoying. In an emergency, when the horse must be evacuated quickly, that can be disastrous. A good solution is the "Blocker Tie Ring." It's a round metal ring with a tongue around which the rope loops. The ring fastens to the existing fixture for tying ropes in the trailer. There are no knots involved. It allows a comfortable and safe degree of slack. There is no danger of accidentally trapping the horse.

*Leg wraps, shipping boots, or bare?* Adding wraps or boots provides more support for the horse's lower legs, particularly on long trips. Boots are easy to fit and adjust. Wraps, however, must be applied properly. If too tight, they can cause circulation problems. Too loose, and they may come undone while traveling. In addition, some horses dislike either form of support and will fuss, kick, stomp, and try to remove them.

## Comfort and Safety for All

Plan your route with comfort and safety for both you and your horse in mind. In general, veterinarians recommend stopping every four hours for 30 minutes to an hour. This gives your horse a break from constantly making the tiny adjustments to compensate for the trailer's movement, not to mention that you also need a break to stay alert and avoid highway hypnosis. When you stop, be aware that many people think you are a mobile petting zoo and might stroll over to "see the horsey" with their kids, even when you are not around. It's a smart idea to lock the trailer door when you leave the trailer unattended for any reason.

Some people don't like traveling during the day in the summer, particularly when temperatures hover near triple digits. If there is good airflow through the trailer, the horse is probably okay. However, when it is scorching, the horse's sweat could evaporate from the airflow. If conditions inside the trailer are a worry, fasten a thermometer to the inside of the trailer and adjust your travel plans to compensate. You can buy a battery-powered fan to rig up in the trailer.

Consider installing a camera to monitor your horse in the trailer. The camera is mounted inside the trailer and sends the image to a monitor mounted on your dashboard. There are several options: some are battery-powered, while others require connecting the system to your tow vehicle's power supply. Some offer night vision capabilities. Others have an option to use the camera as a backup camera for your tow vehicle, and then place it in the trailer when you hit the road.

Monitor your horse's vital signs at each rest stop. Check temperature, pulse, and respiration. Do a capillary check for dehydration. Adjust sheets, blankets, and ventilation as needed. If he seems stressed, listen for gut noises and signs of colic. Never, never, never take your horse off the trailer until you have reached your destination. Not at a rest stop. Not at a public park. Not in a parking lot. Not unless you are okay with the possibility of your spooked horse cantering down the highway, slamming into a vehicle, or grazing on grass that's probably been sprayed with pesticides and has cigarette butts, dog droppings, and broken glass in it. If you must remove the horse for some reason, try to find a stop at a fairground, stable, or farm along your route. Some tack shops have areas where customers can try out tack and they may let you unload there. You can use the online directories of stables which welcome transients. Most of them are close to interstates and other roads often used by traveling horse-people. Download a list of all of the stables along your route in case you need a quick change of plans.

Plan your route with weather, traffic, and destination in mind. If possible, try to go through high-traffic areas in off-peak hours. Driving a horse trailer on a crowded beltway during rush hour is an experience that is best avoided! Consider 8 to 10 hours a full day's drive. In general, you will cover about 50 miles in an hour. That factors in stops for restroom breaks, getting gas, eating, and giving you both that vital 30 to 60 minutes of rest. You'll cover even less ground and should probably make a shorter day of it if you are uncomfortable driving in the dark or have vision impairments, especially if your route includes unlit, poorly marked, or winding roads.

### When You Get There

When you arrive at your destination, monitor your horse's condition. Hand-walk him to relieve stiffness and allow him to graze if he seems comfortable. Give his legs a rub-down with liniment. If you are overnighting at a stable with other transient horses, try to stall your horse away from them. Make sure the bedding is fresh and use your own water and feed buckets. Give him time to recover. The equine center at the University of California at Davis says a horse needs a full day of rest after he has traveled 6 to 12 hours. It can take as long as a week to fully recover from a longer journey.

## TRIP PLANNING

Once you are comfortable with your ability to deal with the practicalities, you can finally start to think about the fun part of the trip. What is it that you want to do? Do you have a wish list of adventures? Ride in all the National Parks or visit every Civil War battlefield that has horse trails? Follow the tracks of cattle drives or wagon trains? Canter on the beach with the descendants of Misty of Chincoteague? Ride and camp in the back country? Now is the time to daydream and research. You've waited a lifetime to plan this, and you deserve to do so without reservations. Create your ultimate muck bucket list!

While many people have been traveling with their horses for years, it's an entirely new adventure for new-to-horses seniors. The challenge of caring for a horse away from the comforting routine of the stable, finding your way to unfamiliar locations, and meeting new people ranks very high on the "way outside of my comfort level" list.

Happily, you'll find plenty of advice to help you. There are dozens of social media groups and pages dedicated to the "happy trails lifestyle." Several of them have a large membership of senior riders. Informal local groups often trailer out on weekends; others are regional clubs that organize longer outings for many members. Browse the groups and websites to find the ones that give you the best information about the practicalities of horse camping, recommendations of trails and campgrounds, and networking with other campers. You will probably connect with people before you hit the road, and have a list of stopovers, campgrounds, activities, and people which is very reassuring. (A list of the current and active groups is on www.ridersofacertainage.com.)

One way to ensure a successful, stressfree trip is to be well-prepared by addressing as many variables as possible before pulling away from the stable. As mentioned earlier, start by estimating the time it will take to reach your destination. When you factor in stops for gas, food, stretching your legs, and using restrooms, you will cover about 50 miles every hour if you are on an interstate, less if you are using secondary roads. For peace of mind, top off your gas tank when it hits halfway. That way, if you must detour or get stuck in a traffic jam or find yourself in a "gas station desert," you won't worry about running on empty.

Join a roadside assistance insurance plan that covers equestrians. Roadside coverage from most auto insurance companies and companies like AAA and Good Sam will not respond to emergencies involving trailers or horses. There are three roadside service plans that cover equine travel: HaulSafe, Trailguard, and USRider. Their policies cover on-the-road breakdowns and roadside emergencies involving trailers. If the problem cannot be fixed on site, they will transport the trailer to a repair facility (with the horses on board if necessary), arrange overnight accommodations for horses and you, and provide some coverage for veterinary care if needed. All three of those companies (and many other equine associations and organizations) offer discounts for hotels and restaurants that are useful when traveling.

For overnight trips, arrange for stops in advance. There are several online directories of stables that offer overnight accommodations. Fairgrounds and State and National Parks are also good possibilities. Online "travel groups" often post queries for recommendations for stops along a route and reviews of campgrounds and accommodations. Use the online accommodations directories to download a list of every stable and overnight possibility along your route. You now have options if your plans change, and you need to stop somewhere other than where you originally planned. (Links to the current, active directories are at www.riders-ofacertainage.com.)

Program your GPS for your route before you hit the road. Contact your destination to make sure the GPS address is correct. Sometimes, it is not recognized by the system or the driving directions are roundabout and inaccurate. You don't want to discover that when you are lost on a strange back road in the rain at night.

I've mentioned the value of a CB before. Cell phones are nice, but they don't work everywhere, and they can't warn of an accident down the road or provide a detour around it. Truckers are an excellent advance warning system for traffic tie-ups, construction, and accidents. They use Channel 19. Give yourself a CB "handle" like "Silver-Haired Cowgirl!" If you have a problem, truckers are the "knights of the road" and will help you. State Police also monitor specific CB frequencies, either Channel 77 or Channel 47.

# PART SEVEN

## FAMILY AND FINANCES

# Money and Manure:
# Finances of Life—and Horses

**M**ost of us would rather scrub out slimy water troughs than balance our checkbooks or navigate our financial plans. But getting a handle on our finances is vital, especially as we get older. Finances are a sobering topic. As tedious as it seems, developing a financial plan for our pre-and post-retirement years can prevent a crisis that can end not only your horse-related dreams but ruin your entire retirement life.

Few pastimes are as non-economical as horses. Whatever your riding goals, there is a price tag, and it is guaranteed to be higher than you anticipated. Money is always the limiting factor in the horse world. If you want an affordable hobby, you should take up cross-stitching.

If riding is going to be a casual activity, finances are probably not a significant issue. You know what lessons cost, and you've juggled the numbers to know what you can afford. If your current plan is to take a few lessons a month and buy just enough gear to get by, you are probably fine. But horses are addictive, so whatever those figures are, they will change with every ride or visit to a tack store. You'll soon be thinking about riding more often, maybe starting serious training, either for competition or just to improve your skills. The notion of owning your own horse becomes more attractive with each lesson. This means budgeting for boarding, vet, and farrier services, as well as a saddle, bridle, and tack. If the lure of winning ribbons tempts you, there are registration fees, transportation, stabling, food, and possibly hotels.

Seriously determined to progress? Add in the costs of clinics and—if you are resolute—wintering at Wellington under the tutelage of a dressage professional or attending courses in Texas taught by well-known trainers or natural horsemanship experts. If horse camping and exploring trails around the country is your dream, you'll need a trailer and a proper tow vehicle. And many of us long to buy a piece of land and keep our horses in the backyard, which adds another dimension to the phrase "stable finances."

Our income, expenses, earning potential, and ability to adjust to changing personal, physical, and financial situations shift drastically in our near and post-retirement years. When we retire, our monthly income will probably change as our paychecks stop and we rely on pensions and investments. This change profoundly affects all aspects of our lives, not just our involvement with horses.

Post-retirement income depends on savings, Social Security, investments, pensions, and possibly finding another job. According to the Census Bureau, most of us retire at age 63. We will probably live another 20 years. The old, general rule was that you needed between 70 to 80 percent of your pre-retirement income to maintain the same standard of living you had before retirement. This is now considered optimistic, partly because of rising costs, partly because of longer lifespans, and partly because we are more active and, therefore, spend more.

The time to start planning for retirement is yesterday. Financial experts say pre-retirement planning should begin when you are in your forties or early fifties at the very latest. Many of us have missed that deadline by a decade or more. Even if you are older and think you don't have the investments or savings to justify working with a professional, set up a meeting with a financial planner. She'll review your current financial situation, including savings, debts, income, monthly expenses, mortgage, other financial obligations, expected income from Social Security, pensions, 401(k)s, and other investments. She'll make recommendations and help you set up a plan.

Whether you choose to work with a planner or not, evaluate your monthly and annual expenses. Go back for a year. List everything with the thoroughness of an

## *Analyze Your Financial Future*

➤ Once you finish your budget review, consider your current income and what happens as you get older.

➤ If you are still working, is your employment solid? Is the company solvent? Is it likely to be outsourced or downsized?

➤ Might you be "downsized" because of your age? It's not legal, but it happens. What are your employment prospects if you are let go?

➤ If you are offered an early retirement or severance package, does it compensate for your lost future income? Is it likely you will find another job paying close to what you were making? Will another job have benefits or a pension plan?

➤ What happens if the economy crashes? If this happens when you are in your forties or even fifties, there is enough time for savings and investments to recover. In our sixties and older, not so much.

➤ What do you have in savings?

➤ What are your debts and obligations, both now and in the future? Include the expected things, like replacing your car, and the unexpected, like medical bills.

IRS auditor on a caffeine high. You'll be startled at how much you spend and what you spend it on. Then it is simple math. Subtract your essential monthly expenses—housing, transportation, utilities, food, clothing, insurance premiums, medical expenses, credit card payments, auto loans—from your monthly income. What's left is the disposable income you can spend on non-essentials: travel, eating out, entertainment, and—the most important item—horses.

If you find wasteful spending (and you will), cut it out. Decide which things are essential and which you won't notice if they are gone. Some things cannot be

## AGELESS ADVICE

➤ Could you take out a home equity loan in an emergency? Would you be able to pay it back with your current income?

➤ Is there a second income? Is that needed to meet the monthly bills, or is it the extra that allows for luxuries like riding? What happens if that income stops? We are on the downside of the bell curve chronologically, and women usually outlive their husbands. So, what happens if his income stops? Are there insurance, survivor benefits, or pensions?

➤ What is your medical coverage? Does your medical insurance cover horseback riding? Some plans consider riding an "extreme" sport, resulting in higher premiums or uninsurability. Usually, "extreme" means things like bronco riding or performing in a circus, but you need to check.

➤ Do you have a "catastrophic" or "long term" insurance policy? Such a policy covers nursing homes, assisted living, in-home nursing care, and treatment for catastrophic injuries. The policies can cost several thousand dollars a year, but a month of long-term care costs more than the annual premium.

➤ If you are not yet eligible for Medicare, how much of a strain are your current insurance premiums and deductibles?

➤ If you are on Medicare, can you cover the things not covered by the plan or private supplemental insurance?

eliminated. Replacing a refrigerator that has cooled its last gallon of milk is necessary. But what about other expenses? Do you really need to trick out your house for every holiday? How much do you spend on streaming services that you rarely watch? Add up the "nice but not necessary" number. It can easily be several months of boarding fees or the cost of annual vaccinations.

It is easy for things to overwhelm you financially if you are unprepared. That can lead to the heartbreak of selling your horse and giving up riding. On the other hand, having your financial situation under control means you can budget for your horses and know precisely how much you can spend on them now and what you'll be able to afford in the future.

# CHAPTER 23

# Dealing with an Unsupportive Spouse

You come home from the barn bubbling with excitement. You trotted today. Trotted! And then you and your barn buddies went on a trail ride. Nothing much, just once around the perimeter of the pastures. And you discovered that your horse loves watermelon. You must buy some tomorrow on your way to the stable.

You tell this to your husband, eager to share this great day with him. And all you get is a grunt. Or, "When is dinner?" Or, "You and those damn horses." Or, "I don't know how you think we can pay for that." Your happiness deflates like a ruptured balloon.

When riders trade stories about their families and horses, conflict is a common theme. The issue of spousal support or lack of same routinely comes up on social media groups, forums, chat rooms, and gripe sessions at the stable.

Some stories about spouses and horses are wonderful, positive tales of partners accepting our hobby with good—or at least bemused—grace. Significant others might decide to share the adventure. They learn to ride and eventually get their own horses. Then, there are those who don't ride but share the chores, buy equipment, build barns and jumps, learn how to trim hooves, and willingly make economic sacrifices to afford the horses. They learn to hook up and haul a trailer. They help you memorize your dressage tests and reining patterns. They cheer you at horse shows.

Supportive spouses sit through yet another viewing of *The Black Stallion* and have listened to your comments long enough to recognize good and bad riding in movies. Some partners are not enthusiastic but think this is a phase and are happy to let you work this out of your system, figuring that this flame will burn out and you will soon return to normal.

Occasionally, clever women use proactive techniques to win over their spouses and keep them contented while they ride. They organize an "intro to horses" session to teach partners the basics of handling and grooming. They know that many macho men are actually afraid of horses but don't want to admit it. Get them together, and they feed off each other's egos to see who can do the best job of grooming and leading their horse. Finish the day with a cookout and barn party for couples, and new friendships start.

If your significant other doesn't share your excitement, you might just get a wave as you head out the door on your way to the stable. That's most often true when partners have their own hobbies and interests. More often, the stories are of pushback and negativity: dismissive attitudes, complaints about expenses, discovering new responsibilities that require your attention, and general fault-finding that has nothing to do with horses.

That attitude doesn't wait to surface until the relationship is permanent, either. Engagements end when the prospective groom announces that the horses will have to go so that they can buy a house and, if not now, certainly when there are kids. Or first dates being last dates when the love interest dismisses riding and horses as trivial and silly.

Much of the conflict is because horses are more than a hobby. Once you progress beyond weekly lessons, horses become a lifestyle. That's an unexpected and often major shift in the family dynamic. Like horses, people want predictability and routine. While change in our lives is inevitable, it is not always welcome, especially when you are not the one initiating it. The enthusiasm for your new interest can be unsettling. If you've generally had a good relationship with your significant other until now, it's probably not the level of affection that's changed, it's the change itself that's creating the reaction. Your dream of devoting more time to horses disturbs your partner's sense of regularity, well-being, and security. If your spouse reacts with annoyance, these complaints can segue into making you feel guilty about spending time at the stable.

Guilt trips are hard to resist. Our culture teaches us that it is rude for women to say, "No." We grew up in a time and society where women were expected to be submissive. Fulfillment came from meeting others' needs before or instead of "indulging" in ours. Most of our lives are dictated by our obligations as mother, wife, babysitter, income-generator, caretaker, bake-sale organizer, scout leader, choir member, and supporter of everyone else. While we may genuinely enjoy these roles, they often limit opportunities to enjoy our personal interests.

To some extent, we set ourselves up for this. Traditionally a mother takes care of her family. She cooks, cleans, runs errands, does their laundry, helps with school projects, and makes them dependent on her. Studies show that working women spend as much time doing housework as they do at their jobs with little to no help from their significant other.

Add into this scenario the personality changes that working with horses generate for many women. We become independent and self-reliant, attributes that we may not have demonstrated or even known that we possessed before we began this human-horse partnership. We find a new level of self-respect as we learn how to successfully manage and function in an unfamiliar environment. We are more willing to speak our minds, stand up for ourselves, and pursue our interests even if they conflict with other people's plans. This can be a massive shift in how we think, act, and live, which can unnerve your partner if you've always been the passive, compliant help-mate.

Age may be another element. If your spouse is also nearing retirement, everything about his life, career, finances, and health is changing, too. Experts say that we should start designing our retirement three to five years before we pack up our desks, clear out our locker, and drive out of the parking lot for the last time.

Not everyone follows this schedule. Many people define their identities by their jobs and their status as income-earners, if not the breadwinners in a relationship. This is the source of their self-esteem. They might look at retirement as a reward for years of labor but haven't considered what that reward should be. That's especially true if they had positions of importance in their old jobs and never developed other interests. Loss of identity and status, feelings of uselessness, and loss of social contact are the most common complaints among retirees.

By and large, women follow the pre- and post-retirement "schedule" more closely and eagerly than men. We are already involved in family, community, and social activities, so we look at retirement as a chance to devote more time to the things we enjoy and that satisfy us. When horses are a significant part of that dream, we might already be taking riding lessons and perhaps wondering if we should move to a more horse-centric area. If our partners haven't expressed any plans of their own, we might assume that they are content with going along with our ideas.

Add all these elements together, and it is not surprising that some spouses react with angry, controlling behavior. If it is strong and continuous, you might decide that the "peace" of ending the negative pressure and hassle is worth the disappointment and frustration of not fulfilling your desires. You sigh, cry, and give up riding.

Counselors and psychologists say this is a bad response. You might comply, but you will resent it even if you don't acknowledge it. You will resent the people who forced you to give in. You'll resent having to do things that keep you away from your interests, especially when others are not making similar concessions. You'll resent that your sacrifice is expected as a mandatory obligation without recognition or appreciation. Your anger will build, your attitude will sour, and your relationship will deteriorate.

Between your anger and resentment and the tension from dealing with your partner's attitude, you can quickly spiral into depression. Therapists say that an unsupportive spouse is a primary source of depression. Almost half of the couples in therapy have at least one depressed spouse. And it is contagious, with the problems of one spouse leading to similar problems for the other.

Psychologists say that controlling behavior is often a symptom of depression that stems from a sense of emotional fragility and vulnerability. Controlling behavior gives someone a sense of autonomy over a situation. Complaints about horses are a symptom, not a cause. It is a form of "the best defense is a good offense." Psychologists list 20 different signs of controlling behavior. These include some of the most commonly mentioned attitudes of horse-hating spouses, like chronic criticism, guilt trips, ridiculing or teasing with a nasty undercurrent, thwarting your goals by making you doubt yourself, not respecting your need for personal interests, and making affection conditional on your accommodating him.

Communication is the first step in trying to solve the problem. A familiar proverb claims that a good marriage is a never-ending series of conversations and compromises. Sometimes, all that is needed is a heart-to-heart conversation, either by just the two of you or with a counselor or therapist to steer the conversation and serve as a referee, if needed.

Tell your partner how much horses mean to you and that you don't want to live your life regretting not trying something you've dreamed of. Point out that after spending years fulfilling obligations to the family, you've earned this. Explain that spending time with horses is a great stress reliever and cheaper than a therapist.

If you are under the pre-retirement years' umbrella, now is the time to discuss what retirement means for both of you. What do you want to do and where do you want to live? Horses may be part of the conversation, but it should be broader than that.

When partners have no interest in horses, they can easily feel left out and abandoned. They might be shy about meeting new people or spending time in an unfamiliar setting. If you have children or are a caregiver, your spouse may feel the time and attention you give to horses affect your obligations in that area. Legitimately, there may be concern about the possibility of injury. Checkbook issues will undoubtedly come up.

Work to find solutions and compromises. Find ways to be involved in each other's lives. Maybe you agree to spend one weekend at the stable and the next doing what your partner wants. Invite both old and new friends to parties and expand your social circle. If you've been the primary housekeeper, it's time to share the household chores and shopping or hire a housecleaner. If there are kids still living at home, they can also carry more of the household chores.

Ideally that approach works, and you achieve détente, if not total acceptance and peace. But that's not always the case. According to the Center for Disease Control, roughly 50 percent of marriages end in divorce. Financial disagreements and money problems are the number one cause. Poor communication, abuse, losing interest in each other, and infidelity are also on the list. The devotion to horses can be a factor that highlights weak areas in a relationship. Unhappy partners sometimes claim that the horse is more important than the spouse, so perhaps "infidelity"— with the horse being the "other party"—isn't too far off the mark.

In addition to the mental health problems, being in an unhappy marriage also has physical consequences. Women in unsupportive or tumultuous relationships suffer more cases of high blood pressure and heart disease, eating disorders, weaker immune systems, and longer recovery times from illnesses, injuries, or surgery. Studies find that living in an unhappy marriage is more dangerous to your health than living in isolation. People who choose to be single have better mental health than those staying in unhappy relationships. That is a fundamental change in assumptions about lifestyles, which held that living alone led to depression.

If you can't compromise, if the criticism and negativity never end, if you never want to leave the barn and dread being at home, if you want to keep the relationship alive but feel that you have done all that you can on your own, find a counselor, even if you go by yourself. A professional can help you assess your situation in both the emotional and practical sense and help you decide about staying or leaving.

Therapists recommend pulling together a group of friends and confidants for support and advice. Practice good self-care by eating, exercising, sleeping, and creating private time to regroup. Appreciate that you'll have mixed feelings; it's hard to consider ending a relationship to which you've devoted years of your life, energy, and dreams. When you've done all that, you'll be able to make a decision that you can live with.

# CHAPTER 24

# Protecting Your Horse When You Are Gone

## WILLS, TRUSTS, AND OTHER END-OF-LIFE PLANS

It is unpleasant to realize, but we are on the downside of the bell curve of life. Planning for the inevitable end of our lives is not a pleasant task but knowing that we've done what we can to prepare for it gives us peace of mind. We know that our wishes will be carried out and that where our horse is concerned, he will be cared for.

Everyone needs an estate plan. This includes a will and possibly a trust. This paperwork spells out the distribution of your property and money, makes sure that all bills and taxes are paid, and deals with things like providing for the care of your horse. As part of your planning, it is advisable also to have a Living Will and a Power of Attorney. These two documents operate before death. A Living Will allows you to direct what will happen in the case of a severe or terminal illness or condition. You also can appoint a health care surrogate to make medical decisions for you when you are no longer able to do so. The Power of Attorney allows you to appoint someone who will handle business and financial matters should you become unable to manage them.

Many people think that they do not have enough assets to require a will or establish a trust. However, if you die "intestate"—the legal term for without a will—everything you have will pass as dictated by state statute, not as you might choose. Your heirs have no control over what happens to any of it. Without legal written instructions, the courts will dispose of your property as dictated by statute. This is particularly important when your estate owes bills, taxes, or has other financial obligations. Despite your desires, your horse (and barn and trailer and tack) will be disposed of in the interests of your creditors. Legally, your horse is just another asset to be sold off, like your car or your house. If the fastest and easiest way to settle your estate is to take your horse to auction, that may well happen.

The immediate concern about what happens after your death is the care for your horse until the legal process takes over. In a boarding situation, this is easy since the routine care will probably not change. However, if you board at home or in a self-care situation, you must make sure that someone can step in and has the funds to provide the necessary care. This could be the person named in your Power of Attorney. Discuss the possibility with that person and determine where the money will come from.

If you've made no long-term arrangements for your horse, his fate may not be a happy one. Online horse groups post pleas almost daily for horses needing new homes because their owners have died or can no longer care for them. Non-riding family members may decide just to give the horse away or sell it cheaply. If your instructor, barn manager, or a riding friend oversees that action, it might turn out well, particularly if they have contacts in the local horse community. On the other hand, a horse sold cheaply or given away to strangers may be a horse that does not go to its "forever home" but to an auction.

Rehoming is particularly difficult if your horse is old or has difficult medical conditions. Often, people think that an equine rescue will take an aging, ill, or ownerless horse, but that is rarely the case. Rescues are stretched to their limits both with physical resources and financial ability and may not be able to add another horse to their herd, particularly if it has special and expensive needs. Most have strict guidelines about which horses they will accept, and do not have the option of expanding those requirements.

Some equine retirement centers accept horses, particularly if there is money to help cover the cost of their care, but they also have requirements that your horse might not meet. Those centers are also often full. Donating a horse to a school with an equine studies program or a therapeutic riding center is another option if your horse suits their needs, which are often very specific.

If the other options fall through, sometimes euthanasia is a kinder choice for an aging, ill, or infirm horse than seeing him go to auction or end up at a place where he is neglected or abused.

The best way to guarantee that your horse is cared for the way you want is to draw up a will or a trust and appoint an executor or trustee who will make sure your wishes for your horse's care are complied with.

*Wills* and *trusts* are two different things. A *will* is a set of instructions that spell out how you want your belongings and assets to be distributed. The instructions are carried out as soon as possible under the supervision of an executor. However, those instructions are not carried out, and the money and possessions not distributed until the will has gone through probate. That's a legal process that ensures all debts and taxes owed are paid in full before the assets are distributed. It can take several months to several years.

A popular option is to leave your horse to someone in your will. This often includes a bequest of money or property to cover the costs of caring for your horse. If you haven't made other arrangements, whoever inherits your horse is responsible for all the expenses until the will is probated, which, as mentioned, could take years. Legally, the executor of the estate is responsible for the physical condition of assets until the will is through probate. The money in the estate pays for that. In most cases, this means maintaining the condition of a house or vehicles. In your case, it would include ensuring the horse is cared for until probate is concluded and the rest of the money is available. However, there is always the chance that the expenses are higher than expected or unknown debts appear, and the estate is drained of funds. This leaves nothing to cover the costs of caring for your horse before, during, or after probate. When this happens, whoever inherits your horse also inherits all the bills.

A more secure way of providing for your horse is a *trust*. Every state and the District of Columbia have pet trust laws. A trust legally arranges for the care of your horse in the event of your death or disability. You determine the amount of money needed to cover the expenses of your horse's care and name a trustee to oversee the management of the trust. One advantage of a trust over a will is that a trust does not go through probate, which means the money from your estate is available immediately. The trustee can be anyone you choose, but it is often a lawyer or a financial manager. Another advantage is that often you can change the terms of a trust more easily than you can change your will.

With a trust, your assets are distributed over time, from a few months to many years. A typical example of a trust is a teenager who inherits money from his grandparents, but the trust limits how much he receives each year and what he can do with it. In the case of animals, a trust usually provides support for the remainder of the animal's life. When you hear about the crazy cat lady who leaves a million dollars to Fluffy to continue living in the late owner's mansion and being fed lobster three times a week for the rest of her life—that's a trust.

The terms of a trust can be as general as paying someone a specified amount to care for the horse with no further instructions or can be very detailed: where the horse is boarded, who can ride it, feed requirements, dealing with health and aging issues, and whether it can be sold, down to the color and brand of its turnout sheet. You must provide identification of your horse through microchips, DNA, or another method as protection against fraud. The trustee can require regular inspections to guarantee that your instructions are being followed.

The trust also spells out what happens to any money left over after the horse dies. Many lawyers recommend that the funds go to a charity or some beneficiary not associated with the trustee. As horrible as it sounds, there are cases of people neglecting or euthanizing animals in their care in order to get leftover money from a trust.

Both wills and trusts require registration and ownership papers and medical records. These are necessary for assessing the value of the estate as well as the horse's value if the will or trust allows it to be sold. Make sure ownership papers are up to date.

There are many ideas about preparing a will without using a lawyer. Their legality depends on many conditions. Check with your state's Office of Register of Wills to determine the requirements for writing a valid, legal will. The office is usually found on your state's government website.

Some people turn to online legal websites or "fill in the blank" templates, especially if they think they don't have enough assets to justify working with a lawyer to draw up a will or trust. These are not good options. The forms are very general and often do not cover things you might not know you need to consider. They do not allow the personalization and specific instructions you may want. In addition, each state has its own legal tweaks, which these forms don't address.

Another idea that pops up is to write your will, sign it, and mail it to yourself by registered mail. This may not be legal. In most states, the will must be signed by two witnesses in the presence of each other. Some localities also require that a Notary Public witness the signing.

There are states that accept handwritten wills. These are called "holographic" wills. Visit the Register of Wills website in your state to learn what the particular requirements are for their legality. In 2021, the states that accepted them were:

Alaska, Arizona, Arkansas, California, Colorado, Idaho, Kentucky, Louisiana, Maine, Michigan, Mississippi, Montana, Nebraska, New Jersey, North Carolina, North Dakota, Pennsylvania, South Dakota, Tennessee, Texas, Utah, Virginia, West Virginia, and Wyoming. A few states accept hand-written wills from service members stationed overseas, while others refuse to accept them under any circumstances.

If you have not had to settle an estate, you will be stunned at how much paperwork is involved. Unfortunately, most people do not thoroughly organize their files and papers. That leaves a burden on family or others who must deal with these practicalities while mourning your passing. Buy a "When I'm gone" workbook to help you organize your paperwork and other information. This includes a list of business, professional, financial, and personal contacts (you probably have many friends and acquaintances that those settling your estate do not know); location of legal, medical, and financial documents; list of loans to be paid and debts owed to you; household items destined for specific individuals; and instructions for your horse and other pets.

Buy an "address" book designed to record all of your computer and internet information: websites, usernames, URLs, and passwords. Lack of access to email, banking, credit card, and other accounts complicates settling affairs.

Transfer all this information onto a "Letter of Last Instruction." This is not a legal document, but it spells out your instructions and desires. It speeds up the process of settling your estate, especially in the area of things that need immediate attention. Sign and date the letter. You should update this every year. Store it in your safe deposit box with other important papers. Give copies of the letter to your attorney, CPA or financial advisor, family members, and anyone else who needs that information immediately. (A link to a Letter of Last Instruction form is found at www.ridersofacertainage.com.)

Where your horse is concerned, list your intentions very precisely, even if these are covered by your will or a trust. Specify who will care for your horse; who pays the bills for board and veterinary care; how much will be paid and when; where that money will come from; how long that will continue; whether the caretaker can sell the horse or become its owner; the conditions under which that can happen; what happens if the caretake cannot continue to take care of the horse. Add other concerns or instructions you want to address. Be as specific as possible. Have everyone involved read the document, adjust it as necessary, and sign it. You then have peace of mind that your partner is safe.

# The Trail Never Ends

R*iders of a Certain Age* started as a lark. I planned it as a fun romp through the world of adult amateur women learning dressage. I'd write about taking lessons, learning dressage tests, and looking for a horse, all with a lot of tongue-in-cheek banter. There'd be a lot of fun trivia like what the letters around the dressage arena mean and Trigger's other screen credit (Maid Marian's horse in *Robin Hood*, 1938). I never thought it would be anything substantial.

But then I joined social media groups for older women riders and quickly realized that my vision was too narrow and superficial. With every hour I spent scrolling through conversations, I found women asking for advice about another pertinent topic or starting a conversation about a subject I'd never considered. As I read the comments and researched the issues, I added more and more information to my notes and another section to the manuscript.

At some point, any writer has to say, "Enough!" I needed to winnow down the material. The medical sections read like a textbook, and there was more advice on healthy living than the entire self-help section at Barnes and Noble. Horse training advice, navigating the Social Security system, and surviving as a caregiver are important topics for us but are far too involved to address in a handbook for older novices discovering the equestrian lifestyle.

Even as I was finishing the manuscript, I was still finding bits and bobs to add to the existing material. It's never-ending, but that's what learning about horses is— no matter what you know or think you know, there's always more to learn. The best riders and horsewomen realize that and continue learning and finding new ways to expand their horse-oriented lives. They do so for the sheer joy of the experience: developing a deeper connection with their horse, meeting the challenge of trying a new skill, working through a scary moment, and tricking themselves out in new duds, all the while making new friends with which to share the memories.

There's a song in the musical *Pippin* called "No Time at All." In the play, Pippin, the son of Charlemagne, is searching for the meaning of life. He visits his grand-mother, who sings about her philosophy. "Here is a secret I never have told; maybe you'll understand why. I believe if I refuse to grow old, I can stay young till I die." I think that attitude is one reason why so many of us "Riders of a Certain Age" are in the saddle at 50, 60, 70, 80, and beyond.

I truly hope we meet on the trail, in the arena, or at a clinic. In the meantime, saddle up, and always have fun!

# RESOURCES

**W**hat follows is a selection of resources for all riders of a certain age. I've included names and web addresses of organizations, businesses, and social media groups mentioned in this book (Facebook groups or pages are identified by **FB** preceding the entry). The information is current as of writing; however, things change rapidly in the equine world. New products and information become available, and existing sources go out of business. Social media groups disband while new groups become the "go-to" site for conversation and advice. Because of that, the information here is rather general. In a few cases where a specific company fills a very limited niche, it is mentioned. Note that inclusion or mention *does not mean a recommendation*. It is just information.

For a far more extensive and frequently updated offering of resources, please visit the online companion to this book, www.ridersofacertainage.com, and the Facebook page and group of the same name. There you'll find the latest news, product information, and links to useful sites.

## Finding Other Riders of a Certain Age

Over a dozen groups on Facebook and MeWe are specifically for older women riders. While most are general in scope, some groups focus on trail riding, others traveling with your horse; there are grief support groups for those who have lost their horses, pages for people dealing with fear, and gatherings of followers of specific disciplines or trainers. You can easily spend days browsing through them. A current list is on www.ridersofacertainage.com.

You can also search for horse groups on Meetup. This is a platform that connects people with similar interests in a specific geographic area.

Ask a Veterinarian and Horse Vet Corner are two Facebook groups that allow people to ask veterinary questions. Only approved veterinarians are allowed to respond. An auxiliary group—HVC-Coping with the Loss of a Horse Support Group—helps members deal with the death of their riding partner and friend.

## Having Horses, Not Riding

(FB) The Non-Ridden Equine
(This is the Facebook page created by Victoria Yates for those interested in non-riding relationships with their horses.)

The International Horse Agility Club
www.thehorseagilityclub.com
(FB) The International Horse Agility Club

EAGALA (Equine Assisted Growth and Learning Association) www.EAGALA.org
(FB) EAGALA Network
(There are also several EAGALA FB groups for geographic areas.)

Equine Experiential Education Association
https://e3assoc.org
(FB) Equine Experiential Association

Association for the Advancement of Natural Horse Care Practices
www.aanhcp.net
(FB)Paddock Paradise Track System

*Horse Speak, Horse Training in Translation,* and *Essential Horse Speak: Continuing the Conversation*
(FB) SharonWilsie
(Books and teachings from Sharon Wilsie that show us how to use body language to communicate with horses.)

## Finding an Instructor

The Certified Horsemanship Association
www.cha.horse
(FB) Certified Horsemanship Association

American Riding Instructors Association
www.riding-instructor.com
(FB) American Riding Instructors Association

US Hunter Jumper Association
www.ushja.org
(FB) United States Hunter Jumper Association – USHJA

Centered Riding
www.centeredriding.org
(FB) Centered Riding

US Dressage Federation
www.usdf.org
(FB) United States Dressage Federation Official Page

British Horse Society
www.bhs.org.uk
(FB) The British Horse Society

## Learning Horsemanship and How to Ride

These are the largest and most well-known of the horse expos in the United States, but there are many more regional events worth exploring. The websites have details about the clinicians, the schedule of demonstrations, and special events at the shows. The Facebook groups have last-minute information.

Equitana
www.equitanausa.com
(FB) EquitanaUSA

Equine Affaire
www.equineafffaire.com
(FB) Equine Affaire, Inc (Official)
(There are two Equine Affaires. One is held in Columbus, Ohio. The other is in West Springfield, Massachusetts. The website is for both events.)

Western States Horse Expo
www.horsexpo.com
(FB) Western States Horse Expo

Horse World Expo
www.horseworldexpo.com
(FB) World Horse Expo

University of Guelph Online Courses
www.thehorseportal.ca
(While there are many online courses and seminars, the ones offered by the University of Guelph consistently rank among the most professional and affordable.)

## Fitness

These books consistently appear on the top of the list for professional, credible fitness training. In addition to these titles, look for online videos by these authors.

*Fitness, Performance, and the Female Equestrian* by Mary Midkiff

*The Rider's Fitness Program* by Diana Robbin Dennis

*The Rider's Pain-Free Back Book* by James Warson, MD and Ami Hendrickson
*Pilates for Equestrians: Achieving the Winning Edge with Increased Core Stability* by Liza Randall

*Pilates for Riders: Align your Spine and Control Your Core for a Perfect Position* by Lindsay Wilcox-Reid

*Yoga for Equestrians* by Linda Benedik and Veronica Wirth

*Equestrian Yoga: Yoga with, on, and for Your Horse* by Danny Chapparo and Natalie DeFee Mendik

*Yoga for Riders: Principles and Postures to Improve Your Horsemanship* by Cathy Woods
The Somatic Systems Institute has a series of audio lessons covering somatic exercises for specific body parts of groups: lower back, hands and wrists, legs and hips, knees and pelvis, jaw and neck, and "protruding belly." These are conducted by Thomas Hanna, the developer of the technique.
www.Somatics.org

## Dealing with Fear

*Riding Fear Free: Help for Fearful Riders and Their Teachers* by Laura Daley and Jennifer Becton is one of the most popular and successful programs. It includes a book, written and physical exercises, and a vast online support network.
https://ridingfearfree.info/
(FB) Riding Fear Free

*The Timid Rider* by Heather Wallace is an ongoing chronicle of one woman's journey from being scared to put her foot in the stirrup to participating in the grueling horse-race across Mongolia.
www.timidrider.com
(FB)The Timid Rider

The late Jane Savoie developed a video program called *Freedom from Fear* for nervous riders that combines motivational actions with riding techniques. This program, as well as the library of her other motivational and instructional books and videos, are available through Trafalgar Square Books.
www.HorseandRiderBooks.com

## Safety

Landsafe
landsafeequestrian.com
(FB) Landsafe-Reducing Rider Risk
(Information about their program and clinic schedule)

Riders4Helmets
(FB) Riders4helmets (This is the international organization raising awareness for the importance of wearing helmets.)

This is a good guide for fitting a riding helmet: https://bit.ly/3qJmcCc

Resistol Ridesafe Cowboy Hats
www.resistol.com

HellHats
(FB) Karen's Hell Hat Posse

ROADiD.com
(Wrist ID bracelet and safety identification tags.)

## Finding a Horse of Your Own

The Right Horse Initiative
www.therighthorse.org
www.myrighthorse.org.

www.unitedhorsecoaltion.org.

## Insurance and Forms

An excellent FAQ from Mize Insurance answers to most common equine insurance questions. And a few not so common.

(Can I insure my reindeer? And, no, the call did not come from Santa.)
www.mize-insurance.com

Power of Attorney and First Responder Forms are found at https://www.usrider.org/travel-safety/transportation-info

## Natural Disasters

The National Equine Emergency Evacuation Directory is a free online resource. It connects people needing to evacuate with a network of volunteers offering stabling, transportation, search and rescue, and other services, like veterinarians and farriers.
www.nationalequineemergencydirectory.com

Fleet of Angels is a national nonprofit organization that provides assistance to horse owners in emergencies. It coordinates with FEMA and national agencies, state emergency offices, and other groups during a crisis to provide accurate information, advice, and effective services.
www.fleetofangels.org

Louisiana State Animal Response Team
https://bit.ly/32hjV7K
(This includes practical information as well as several pages for recording important information.)

*Disaster Planning for You and Your Horse*
https://bit.ly/3GPqHRl
(Excellent in-depth advice and forms for recording everything from Ontario County, New York.)

*Flood, Fire, Earthquake*
https://bit.ly/3FMj24M
(Another good guide—this one from Los Angeles.)

Markel Insurance developed an excellent guide for preparing for hurricanes:
https://bit.ly/3nJ229D

Colorado State
https://bit.ly/3fGrYyb
(Wildfire preparedness.)
University of California at Davis
https://bit.ly/3fGrYyb
(Explain dangers and treatments for horses exposed to wildfire smoke.)

## On the Road

National RV Training Academy
www.nrvta.com
(FB) National RV Training Academy's RV Life Community
(Online and onsite Educated RV Owners Courses.

RVer Insurance Exchange
www.rverinsurance.com
(Clearinghouse of information and sales for medical, Medicare, dental/vision, telemedicine insurance plans for RVers.)

Health Insurance for Full-Time RVers: A Complete Guide. (2019).
*www.fulltimefamilies.com/insurance-for-full-time-rvers/*

Directlabs.com
Healthlabs.com
(Lab tests online.)

Remote Area Medical Volunteer Corps
www.ramusa.org
(FB) Remote Area Medical—RAM
(RAM Telehealth Virtual Medical Appointments. The site also has the schedule of on-site medical clinics.)

Mobile Internet Resource Center
RV Mobile Internet.com
(This site has guides and good information about navigating the often-confusing options and operations for wi-fi, phone, and other connectivity issues. Basic membership is free; paid membership offers many additional benefits.)

HaulSafe: Haulsafe.com
Trailguard: trailguard.org
US Rider: usrider.org
If you need a veterinarian while on the road, the American Association of Equine Practitioners maintains a directory of veterinarians by location: www.aaep.org/horse-owners/get-dvm

## Self-Defense on the Trail

There are many videos and books that address this. These are a few to consider.

Mountedpolice.org
(Bill Ritchey is a retired mounted police officer who, among other things, trains horses that patrol Mardi Gras and has successfully competed in national mounted obstacle course competitions. His weekend-long, de-spooking clinics include training in self-defense on the trail.)

Demonstration by Mike Hughes on YouTube: www.youtube.com/watch?v=JV8hVvnAvIc

Demonstration by Eddie Rodriguez 2012 North American Trail Ride Conference on www.youtube.com/watch?v=Ij5XlNKt1Zo

Horsenation.com/2015/03/31/mounted-self-defense-know-how-to-protect-yourself-on-horseback/ (This is an online article with a video within the story. The audio is difficult to hear, but the video demonstration is good.)

whoapodcast.com/self-defense-trail-riders/
(A podcast with advice and techniques.)

## Finances

Horse Illustrated has a good article on estimating your equine expenses and a budget worksheet: https://bit.ly/3qmj3qH

MyFrugalHome.com has several downloadable budget worksheets for a general monthly budget, tracking auto bill pay and regular monthly bills, and debt repayment.

# REFERENCES

## Buying a Horse

Blocksdorf, Katherine. (2021. April 23). The Best Horse Breeds for First-Time Owners and Riders. *thesprucepets.com*

Cornerstone Equine Academy. How Much Does a Horse Cost? *cornerstoneequineacademy.com*

Cornerstone Equine Academy. (2020. December 4) Questions to Ask When Buying a Horse. *cornerstoneequineacademy.com*

Cornerstone Equine Academy. (2020. November 19). What is a Pre-Purchase Exam and Why Do You Need One? *Cornerstoneequineacademy.com*

Ellerts, Jennie. (2019. May 31). How to Choose the Right Horse for Your Riding Style. *proearthanimalhealth.com*

McVicker, Dee. (2020. December 1). 8 Rules for Buying a Horse. *equusmagazine.com*

Sellnow, Les. (2002. September 1). Horse Auctions: The Good, The Bad, The Ugly. *thehorse.com*

Synergist Saddles. Saddle Fit Concepts. *synergistsaddles.com*

Synergist Saddles. The Narrow Horse and the Heavyweight Rider. *synergistsaddles.com*

Tarr, Judith. (2020. February 10). A Horse for the Larger Rider. *tor.com*

Von Peinen, K. and others. (2010. November 8). Relationship Between Saddle Pressure Measurements and Clinical Signs of Saddle Soreness at the Withers. *Equine Veterinary Journal, Volume 42, Issue s38. P. 650-653.*

Westphalia Ranch. What is a Foundation Quarter Horse? *westphalia-ranch.com*

Wilson, Jayne Pedigo. (2017. March 20) Considerations for the Older Rider. *equisearch.com*

## Economic Impact and Horse Facts

(2017. January 16) The Horse Industry by the Numbers. *Ridewithequo.com*

Brez, Karina. (2021. March 22). 33 Amazing Horse Riding Statistics. *Karinabrez.com*

Equine Business Association. (2018. March 16). The 2017 Economic Impact Study of the US Horse Industry. *Equinebusinessasociation.com*

McGlenn, Michael. (2018. July 20). Graphic illustrations of Economic Impact of Horse Industry in United States. *nwhorsesource.com*

Stowe, PhD, C. Jill. (2018) Results from the 2018 AHP Equine Industry Study. *Americanhorsepubs.org*

## Equine Travel and Lifestyle

Padgett, Alyssa. (2019. December 24). How Much does it Cost to Live in an RV Full-Time? *heathandalyssa.com*

Scheve, Tom and Scheve, Neva. (1998) The Complete Guide to Buying, Maintaining, and Services a Horse Trailer. Howell Book House.

*Equus* (2021. January 28). Shopping for a Towing Vehicle. *Equusmagazine.com*

Coleman, Chris. (2021. April 12). The Breakdown of Living in an RV Full-Time Cost. *rvtalk.net*

Horton, Jennifer. (2017. March 21). Tips on Trailer Living on the Horse Show Road. *equisearch.com*

Equisearch. (2017. March 20). Travelling with Horses. *equisearch.com*

Heath, Brad. (undated). 7 Tips for Safe Overnight Camping with Your Horse. *doubledtrailers.com*

Heath, Brad. (undated). A Guide to Horse Trailer Terminology. *doubledtrailers.com*

Oberdorf, Amy DeGeer. (2021, USRider Safe Travels, Winter). Long-Haul Strategies. https://bit.ly/3fhLX5v

Tips for Getting Medical Care while RVing. (2017. July 11). *thormotorcoach.com*

Trabue, Abigail. (2018. January 12). Healthcare for RVers Solved – Visit a Primary Care Physician Virtually with RV Health. *rvmiles.com*

Health Insurance for Full-Time RVers: A Complete Guide. (2019). *fulltimefamilies.com*

Gray, DVM, MA, Lydia F. (2020). Traveling with Your Horse? Reduce the Red Tape. *aaep.org/horsehealth/traveling-your-horse-reduce-red-tape*

## Family Relationships

Burton, Jonathan. (2019. August 4). You're Probably not Ready to Retire – Psychologically. *MarketWatch.com*

Chen, PhD, Grace. (2016. January 2). My Partner Doesn't Support My Interests. *Drgracechenlmft.com*

Dashnaw, Daniel. (2018. September 13). Unsupportive Spouse Depression. *Couplestherapyinc.com*

Eisenberg, Richard. (2016. April 20). Retirement Life: Women and Men do it Very Differently. *Forbes Magazine*

Gransnet.com Forum. (Undated). How Does Retirement Affect Marriage.

Higgins, Marissa. (2016. August 8). How to Respond when Someone Tries to Guilt You. *Bustle.com*

Johnson MD, Charles Clifford. (1984, October). The Retired Husband Syndrome. *The Western Journal of Medicine*

Nery, Therese. (2017. November 21). I Chose My Horse Over My Husband. *HorseNetwork.com*

Pigg, Cecilia. (2016. November 26). How not to Hate the Hobbies of People You Love. *Aleteia.com*

Shute, Joe. (2017. December 29). Horses for Divorces: why ever more couples are fighting over the family steed. *The Telegraph*

Tan, Alden. (undated). 7 Things to Remember when People Don't Support You. *TineBudda.com*

Taylor, James Michael. (2014. October 5). The Unsupportive Spouse, and Why it's Your Fault. *ThePartTimePhotographer.com*

Uechi, A. (2014. August 7). Horses and Divorce—Just another Statistic? *HorseNation.com.*

Winch, PhD, Guy (2013. May 16). 7 Ways to Get Out of Guilt Trips. Psychology Today.

## Fear

Harrison, Alana. (2019. November 6). Fear of Riding Horses? Here's Your Surefire Solution. *horseandrider.com*

Kennard, PhD, Jerry (2016. May 20). How Fears and Phobia Change as We Age. *healthcentral.com*

Sandoiu, Ana. (2018. June 23). How Horses Perceive and Respond to Human Emotion. *medicalnewstoday.com*

Shemer, Simona. (2015. June 4). Age Dramatically Increases Our Fear of Everything, Study Reveals. *nocamels.com*

Steffanus, Denise. (2019. January 9). Can Horses Really Smell Fear? Yes, and That's Not All. *paulickreport.com*

## Finances

ASPCA. (undated). Pet Trust Laws by State. *Aspca.org*

ASPCA. (undated). Pet Trust Primer. *Aspca.org*

Associa. (undated). HOA101: Rules & Regulations. *Associaonline.com*

Barnett, MSW, Kim. (2020. July 17). Howe to Prepare a Letter of Last Instruction for End-of-Life Wishes. *Agingcare.com*

Investopedia. (undated). Budgeting for the 4 Financial Phases of Retirement. *Investopedia.com*

Merrill, A Bank of America Company. (undated). 7 Steps to Prepare for your Upcoming Retirement. *Merrilledge.com*

Murphy, Meredith. (2020. January 22). The Validity of Handwritten Wills. *Jdsupra.com*

Neumann, Dani. (2020. October 21). I Went to a Financial Planner. They Helped Me Plan for the Horses, too. *Heelsdownmag.com*

Raia, Pat. (2019. April 11). How to Inventory and Insure Your Horse Tack. *Thehorse.com*

Randolph, J.D., Mary. (2021). Holographic Wills. *Nolo.com*

United Horse Coalition. (undated). Estate Planning for Your Horse. *Unitedhorsecoalition.org*

Windhorse Legal, PLLC. (2019. October 1). Horse Trusts. *Horsesandthelaw.com*

## Fitness

Dodd, Katie. (2020. May 21). BMI in the Elderly. *Thegeriatricdietician.com*

Dyson, S., Ellis, A.D. (2019. March 21). The Influence of Ride: Horse Bodyweight Ratio and rider-horse-saddle fit on Equine gait and behavior: A pilot study. *BEVA.onlinelibrary*

Fannin, Blair. (2015. June 15). Study Examines Health Benefits of Horseback Riding. *Agrilifetoday.tamu.edu*

Lawler, Edmund O. (2017. May 18). How to Avoid Crippling Falls After Age 50. *Nextavenue.org*

Melone, CSCS, Linda (2017. June 22). Fitness and Exercise Rules that Change After 50. *Nextavenue.org*

Meyer, Jennifer Forsberg. (2020. Dec. 10). How to be Equestrian Fit.

HorseandRider.com
Meyer, Jennifer Forsberg. (2017. March 20). Tips to Keep Riding Midlife and Beyond. *Equisearch.com*

Minnis, DPT, Gregory. (2020. April 13). The Link Between Weight Loss and Knee Pain. *Healthline.com*

Moors, Debbie. (2012. September). Easing Back In. *Horse & Rider.* *Womenandhorses.com*

National Council on Aging. (undated). Get the Facts on Falls Prevention. *Ncoa.org*

Rodriguez, Diana. (2014. December 17). What's a Healthy Body Weight for Your Age? *Everydayhealth.com*

Stibich, PhD, Mark (2020. June 6). Healthy Weight and BMI Range for Older Adults. *Verywellhealth.com*

The Joint Chiropractic. (undated). Health Benefits of Chiropractic. *Thejoint.com*

Virtual Personal Trainer. (undated). Health and Fitness for Seniors. *Virtual-personaltrainer.com*

Wheeler, MD, Tyler. (2020. January 26). Chiropractic Care for Back Pain. *WebMD.com*.

## Horse Health

American Association of Equine Practitioners. (2015). Chart of Vaccinations for Adult Horses. *Aaep.or.g*

Benton, Kathleen. (2006. Spring). The Effect of Increasing a Rider's Weight on a Horse's Stride. *Trace.tennessee.edu*.

Dodds, DVM, W. Jean. (2013. February 13). Rethinking Equine Vaccinations—Part 1. *ivcjournal.com*.

Dyson, MA, Sue. (2018. March 13). Pilot Study Addresses Effects of Rider Weight on Equine Performance. *Thehorse.com*.

Kentucky Equine Research Staff. (2008. September 15). Horses' Weight-Carrying Ability Studied. *Ker.com/equinenews*.

Lenz, DVM, M.S., DACT Tom. (2021). Signs of a Healthy Horse. *Aaep.org*.

Lesté-Lasserre, MA, Christa. (2020. January 8). Study: Increased Rider Weight Doesn't Significantly Impact Horses. *Thehorse.com*.

Marie, Lisa (2015. October 1). DIY Trailer First Aid Kit. Youtube.com *https://bit.ly/3w7uH9Q*

McFarland, Cynthia. (2015. August 24). The New Equine Deworming Rules. *Horse Illustrated*

National Farm Animal Care Council. (2021) Code of Practice for the Care and Handling of Equines: Euthanasia. *nfacc.ca/codes-of-practice/equine-code#section10*.

National Farm Animal Care Council. (2021) Code of Practice for the Care and Handling of Equines: Five Freedoms. *nfacc.ca/codes-of-practice/equine-code#introduct*.

Nessenson, JD, Ilene. (2016. March 30). Could Your Horse's Vaccines be Causing Harm? *Stretchyourhorse.com*.

Newton, DVM, Mel. (2019. November 14). The Good Death. *Melnewton.com*.

Raia, Pat. (2016. October 19). Why Horses and Senior Citizens are a Great Match. *Horse Illustrated.*

World Horse Welfare (undated). Just in Case—The Facts About Difficult Decisions. Just in Case—The Owners Plan Leaflet. *worldhorsewelfare.org/advice/management/end-of-life.*

### Horse and Human Relationship

Combination Horsemanship. Non-ridden activity generator. *good-horse.com/tools/activity-generator/.*

Emotional Bond between Horses and Humans. *Horseconnection.com.*

Proops, Leanne and others. (2018. May 7). Animals Remember Previous Facial Expressions the Specific Humans have Exhibited. *Current Biology, Vol. 28, Issue 9, p1428-1432.*

Equine Experiential Education Association. *e3assoc.org.*

Izzo, Kim. (2020. September 9). A Different Horse/Human Dynamic: Loved but not Ridden. *Horse-canada.com.*

Raia, Pat. (2019. May 6). Riding Optional: The Non-Ridden Horse. *horseillustrated.com.*

Ryback, MD, Ralph. (2016. July 25). No Horsing Around about the Human-Equine Bond. *psychologytoday.com.*

The International Horse Agility Club. *Thehorseagilityclub.com.*

The Non-Ridden Equine Association UK. *thenonriddenequineassociationuk.org/.*

### Keeping a Horse

Carleigh Fedorka. (2021. February 24). The Business of Boarding. *ayankeeinparis.com.*

Equisearch. (2017. March 20). What You Should Know About Horse Communities. *equisearch.com.*

Hoyt, Jeff. (2018. March 13). Equestrian Retirement Communities. *seniorliving.org.*

O'Meara, Denise Y. (2018. December). A Look at Backyard Horse Keeping. *elcr.org/a-look-at-backyard-horse-keeping/.*

Tyrteos, Alex and Murphy, Katie. (2013, Winter). When Boomers Retire. *eqliving.com.*

Volkenning, Robyn. (2020. April 9). The Hot Trend Where You Live with Your Horses. *horseandrider.com.*

### Mental Abilities and Learning

Breeding, Brad. (2018. May 28). Lifelong Learning: Good for Seniors' Minds and Bodies. *Mylifesite.net.*

CliffsNotes (2020). Physical Development: Age 65+. *Cliffsnotes.com.*

Rebok, PhD, George W. and others. (2014. January 13). Ten-Year Effects of the ACTIVE Cognitive Training Trial on Cognition and Everyday Functioning in Older Adults. *J Am Geriatr Society. 2014 Jan: 62(1): 16-24.*

Howieson, PhD, Diane B. (2015. December 1). Cognitive Skills and the Aging Brain: What to Expect. *Dana.org.*

Steverns, Beth. Center for Medicare Education. (2003). How Seniors Learn. *Mentalhealthpromotion.net.*

## Relationships Around the Barn

Bernstein, Elizabeth. (2020. June 14). Worried About a Difficult Conversation? Here's Advice from a Hostage Negotiator. *Wsj.com.*

Chen, Daryl. (2019. December 16). 3 Steps to Having Difficult—But Necessary—Conversations. *Ideas.ted.com.*

Clawson, Jess. (2019. April 19). Handling Barn Drama: Protecting Your Happy Place. *Theplaidhorse.com.*

Drexler, PhD, Peggy. (2014. August 12). Why We Love to Gossip. *psychologytoday.com.*

Ringer, Judy. (undated). We Have to Talk: A Step-By-Step Checklist for Difficult Conversations. *Judyringer.com.*

Vlietstra, Amanda. (2016. June 2). 6 Dramas that Happen at Every Livery Yard. *HorseandHound.co.uk.*

## Remote Learning

Dopko, Tracy. (2020. May 11). Virtual Coaching: The Socially-Distanced Lesson Solution. *horsesport.com.*

## Safety

Mohney, Gillian. (2016. April 1). Horse Riding is the Leading Cause of Sport-Related Traumatic Brain Injuries, Study Finds. *Abcnews.go.com.*

(2007. February 5). Riding Risks on Par with Car Racing. *Horsetalk.co.nz.*

(2016. January 14) Equestrian Riding Hat Testing. YouTube: https://bit.ly/3blhQZF.

Tafoya, Bernie. (2014. August 28). Tripping Seniors on Purpose to Stop Future Falls. *Chicago.cbslocal.com.*

Bagley, Jennifer. (2018. March 28). Protective Riding Vests: Which One is Right for Me? *Blog/smartpakequine.com.*

Caro, Richard. (undated). Smartwatch as Medical Alert? *Techenhancedlife.com.*

Caro, Richard. (undated). Tutorial: Medical Alert Systems. *Techenhancedlife.com.*

Mansmann, Clare. (2020. August 10). LandSafe is Changing the Way We Think About Falling. *The Chronicle of the Horse.*

Ronan, Amanda Uechi. (2015. March 31). Mounted Self-Defense: Know How to Protect Yourself on Horseback. *Horsenation.com.*

## Showing

Arszman, Megan. (2014. May). Judges Discuss the Dos and Don'ts of Western Fashion. *Gohorseshow.com.*

Equishop. (2020. June 6). How to Choose the Right Riding Gloves. *Equishop.com.*

Hobby Horse Clothing Company. What to Wear for a Show. (Western) hobbyhorseinic.com.

Homoki, Kristal. (2019) Tale of Two Hats—East Meets West. *Westerndressageassocation.org.*

## Women's Health

34 Symptoms of Menopause and what You can do about Them. (undated). *Bodylogic.com.*

American Association of Sleep Medicine. (undated). Sleep and Growing Older. *Sleepeducation.org.*

American Heart Association. (2015. July 31). Menopause and Heart Disease. *Heart.org.*

Bandukwala, DO, Nazia Q. (2020. February 4). Types of Urinary Incontinence. *WebMD.com.*

Brody, Jane E. (2003. September 9). PERSONAL HEALTH (Column): Back in the Saddle, Confident and Diaperless. *The New York Times.*

Driver, MD, Catherin Burt. (2019. December 12). Osteopenia: Causes and Treatment. *Medicinenet.com.*

Gaither, MD, MPH, Kecia. (2019. December 4). Treatment of Menopausal Symptoms. *WebMD.com.*

Harvard Medical School. (2020. August 1). Perimenopause: Rocky Road to Menopause. *Health.harvard.edu.*

Kendal at Home. (2017. June 27). Common Breathing Problems in Older Adults and What You Can do about Them. *Kendalathome.com.*

Kendal at Home. (2016. July 30). 6 Breathing Exercises for Older Adults. *Kendalathome.com.*

Konstantinovsky, Michelle. (2018. July 25). CH-CH-CH-Changes! What to Expect during Perimenopause and Menopause. *Fitbit.com.*

Lewis, MD, David. (undated). Sleep and Aging: Sleep Tips for Older Adults. *Kaiserpermanante.org.*

Mayo Clinic (Undated). Menopause—symptoms and causes. *MayoClinic.org.*

Moawad, MD, Heidi. (2020. December 6). Can Wine Protect Your from Having a Stroke? *VeryWellHealth.com.*

Respiratory Disorders in the Elderly. (2007. February 7). *RTMagazine.com.*

Simon, Stacy. (2020. May 5). 10 Tips to Get More Sleep. *Cancer.org.*

Thorpe, MD, PhD, Matthew. (2017. May 25). How to Fight Sarcopenia (Muscle Loss due to Aging). *Healthline.com.*

US National Library of Medicine. (undated). Aging Changes in the Bones—Muscles—Joints. *Medlineplus.gov.*

Vann, MPH, Madeline R. (2016. August 1). The 15 Most Common Health Concerns for Seniors. *Everydayhealth.com.*

VoicesforPFD.org. (Undated). Bladder Control Factsheet.

# ACKNOWLEDGMENTS

So many people were vital in making this crazy idea become a reality. First, the editors at Trafalgar Square Books who thought it was not so crazy and who gave me the go-ahead to write it. Many thanks to editor Rebecca Didier for her patience and support while dealing with this publishing novice. Then, the stable of friends and professionals who reviewed all or part of the book. They gave me blunt but kind criticism, pointed out errors, corrected grammar and spelling, suggested other areas to investigate, and helped me organize my piles of notes into a functional outline.

Deepest thanks to Diane Cady, Developmental Editor Extraordinaire from Upwork. Peter Ecabert, general counsel of the National Horseman's Benevolent and Protective Association, and John Karas of Karas and Bradford, who reviewed the sections of wills and estate planning and translated legalese into understandable language. Dr. Susan Mende, DVM, of Wolf Creek Equine Hospital in Lothian, Maryland, performed a similar service for the equine health section, helping me include what is most important to horse owners and steering me away from common misconceptions and misinformation. Misty Mize of Jorene Mize Insurance Agency patiently explained the insurance needs of horse owners. Sabine Schleese of Schleese Saddles schooled me on the importance of proper saddle fit and the professional training of saddle fitters. Valerie Pringle of the Humane Society of the United States, Dr. Emily Weiss of the ASPCA, and Ashley Harkins of United Horse Coalition explained the various options for horse buying and the business of kill pens. Stephanie Mills of Horse Dynamics Equine Bodyworks in Charlotte, North Carolina, provided much-needed clarification and support when I was flailing madly and drowning in too much information. The "two Phils" of Anderson Farrier

Service double-checked my views on their world. If there is anything better than knowing one good farrier, it's knowing two, and this father-son tag team is a treasure. Melissa Anderson of Teller, Williams Realty advised me of the many records and requirements new property owners must investigate when starting their farm.

My gang of fellow riders spent their COVID-19 isolation reading drafts of the book and offering suggestions. Aviva Nebesky of Horsepen Hill Farm and co-host of the *Dressage Today* podcast confirmed my instincts about the pacing and length of several sections and brought them under control. Many thanks to Lauren Annett, Amie Blackwell, Jan Brooks, Jane and Jal Dalal, and L.A. Sokolowski. The biscotti was a small payment for the encouragement and insights that you offered. Any errors in factual information or interpretation are entirely mine.

Many companies and individuals graciously allowed me to use their materials and make them available to readers through the www.ridersofacertainage.com website. Markel Insurance; USRider; the University of California at Davis; Ontario County, NY; Large Animal Rescue of Louisiana; Kentucky Performance Products; Hobby Horse Clothes; Bill Richey of National Mounted Police Services; Eddie Rodriguez, and John Harrer of Whoa podcast. The quote from "Pippin" is through arrangement with Alfred Music.

I also owe a debt to the instructors and trainers over the years who have helped me realize my goal of becoming a somewhat competent horsewoman and rider—the late Christine Dodwell, who introduced me to dressage, Karen Rohlf, Christine Nibblett, Kelly Brooke Miller, Aviva Nebesky, Jen Pino, Linda Parelli, and Louise Shively.

As one must have in this digital age, there is a Facebook group and page (Riders of a Certain Age) and a website (www.ridersofacertainage.com). Go there for links to many of the references, products, services, and groups that helped form the base of this book. You'll also find news about developments on subjects in the book, plus useful tips and good stories. That's also where you can post your own experiences. I hope it becomes a community of friends who share the joy of being Riders of a Certain Age. Thank you for reading. Now go ride your horse!

# INDEX